# ECONOMIC IMPACTS OF LAND DEVELOPMENT:

## EMPLOYMENT, HOUSING, AND PROPERTY VALUES

**Thomas Muller**

The research for this report was made possible through a research grant from the Office of Policy Development and Research of the U.S. Department of Housing and Urban Development under the provisions of Section 701(b) of the Housing Act of 1954, as amended, to The Urban Institute. The publication of this report was supported in part by the Ford Foundation. The findings and conclusions presented in this report do not represent official policy of the Department of Housing and Urban Development, the Ford Foundation, or The Urban Institute.

THE URBAN INSTITUTE

Library of Congress Catalog Card Number 76-43223

U.I. 204-214-7

ISBN 87766-173-1

PLEASE REFER TO URI 15800 WHEN ORDERING

Available from:

Publications Office
The Urban Institute
2100 M Street, N.W.
Washington, D.C.   20037

List Price $3.95

Printed in the United States of America

First printing, September 1976

B/77/1500

# FOREWORD

Another report in this series, <u>Fiscal Impacts of Land Development</u>, ex-
plored a number of issues concerning the effect which land use changes
have on governmental revenues and expenditures. This report, also by
Thomas Muller, examines a related set of methodological and data problems regarding the impact of land development on three economic variables in the
private sector: employment, housing, and land values.

The effect of development on each is a concern to government officials
and citizens for two reasons. First, a change in any or all of them contributes
directly to a change in income taxes, property taxes, sales taxes, and a
variety of others. If the difference between these new tax revenues and the
demand for public services and facilities generated by new development is
positive, government is in the enviable position of being able to cut taxes,
expand services, repay debt, or some of each. If the difference is negative,
a rise in taxes, some cut-back in services, or an increase in indebtedness is
the inevitable outcome. Without belaboring the obvious, the effects of development on employment, housing, and land values are of course a concern in their
own right, regardless of their impact on the public fisc, because each plays a
vital part in the individual welfare of households in a community, and therefore, in the welfare of the community as a whole.

As in each of the other reports in this series on the separate and collec-
tive impacts of land development, a many-sided picture emerges on the impacts
which development has on employment, housing, and property values, and how to
estimate them. Muller threads his way through many complex technical issues

in a way which should be helpful to any one trying to arrive at an estimate of the likely economic impact of new development, as well as those trying to gain a fuller appreciation of what constitutes a satisfactory evaluation.

Worth Bateman
Executive Director
Land Use Center
The Urban Institute

# CONTENTS

# ACKNOWLEDGMENTS

This report is part of a broader study sponsored by the Office of Policy Development of the U.S. Department of Housing and Urban Development to evaluate the effects of land development from the local and regional perspective. The encouragement of James Hoben, Program Manager, Division of Community Planning, Development, and Conservation, is appreciated.

Written comments by members of our advisory group were particularly useful, and the advice provided by the group formed the basis for the revision of an earlier draft.

Worth Bateman, Executive Director of the Land Use Center and Franklin James of the Land Use Center staff provided valuable insight which were incorporated into the final report.

# ADVISORY GROUP

Timothy A. Barrow
Mayor
Phoenix, Arizona

Kurt W. Bauer
Executive Director
Southeast Wisconsin Regional Planning
  Commission
Waukesha, Wisconsin

Frank H. Beal
Director for Research
American Society of Planning Officials
Chicago, Illinois

Melvin L. Bergheim
Councilman
Alexandria, Virginia, and National League of
  Cities-U.S. Conference of Mayors

Richard F. Counts
Zoning Administrator
Planning Department
Phoenix, Arizona

Carl D. Gosline
Director of General Planning
East Central Florida Regional Planning
  Council
Winter Park, Florida

Bernard D. Gross
Planning Consultant
Washington, D.C.

Harry P. Hatry
Director
State and Local Government Research Program
The Urban Institute
Washington, D.C.

Ted Kolderie
Executive Director
Citizens League
Minneapolis, Minnesota

Denver Lindley, Jr.
Commissioner
Bucks County
Doylestown, Pennsylvania

Jack Linville, Jr.
Director, Land Management Program
Rice Center for Community Design and Research
Houston, Texas

Alan H. Magazine
Supervisor
Fairfax County Board
Fairfax, Virginia and Project Director
Contract Research Center
International City Management Association
Washington, D.C.

Robert H. Paslay
Planning Director
Planning Commission
Nashville, Tennessee

Richard A. Persico
Executive Director
Adirondack Park Agency
Ray Brook, New York

James R. Reid
Director
Office of Comprehensive Planning
Fairfax County, Virginia

E. Jack Schoop
Chief Planner
California Coastal Zone Conservation
  Commission
San Francisco, California

Duane L. Searles
Special Counsel on Growth and Environment
National Association of Home Builders
Washington, D.C.

Philip A. Stedfast
Planning Director
Department of City Planning
Norfolk, Virginia

David L. Talbott
Director of Planning
Falls Church, Virginia

Richard E. Tustian
Director of Planning
Maryland National Capital Parks and Planning
  Commission
Silver Spring, Maryland

F. Ross Vogelgesang
Director
Division of Planning and Zoning
Indianapolis, Indiana

Thornton K. Ware
Planning Director
Rensselaer County
Troy, New York

Joesph S. Wholey
Member
Arlington County Board
Arlington, Virginia, and Program Evaluation
  Studies Group
The Urban Institute
Washington, D.C.

Franklin C. Wood
Executive Director
Bucks County Planning Commission
Doylestown, Pennsylvania

# GENERAL INTRODUCTION

This report is part of a series of studies on the impacts of land development. It examines the effects of land development on three areas of the economy: employment, housing, and wealth. Since benefits or costs associated with such development generally accrue to individual households, this report complements the study issued in 1975 dealing with the fiscal, or public sector, impact of new development.[1]

The main objective of this report is to provide local governments with inexpensive methods for estimating the impact of new development on the demand for employment and housing. Since both employment and housing effects are regional in nature, regional impacts are also noted. National patterns are shown to provide a basis of comparison between local data and national directions. Most changes in property value tend to occur at the neighborhood level. This is one reason for the comparatively limited interest in this subject at the community or regional level.

The three areas examined in this study--employment, housing, and wealth-- are viewed as one unit for analysis, since each interacts with the others. Additional employment resulting from industrial, commercial, or other development increases the demand for housing. In turn, changes in housing demand affect the value of the existing housing stock and developable land. Residential construction increases the supply of housing and thus affects both

---

1. Thomas Muller, <u>Fiscal Impact of Land Development: A Critique of Methods and Review of Issues</u> (Washington, D.C.: The Urban Institute, 1975).

the price of existing dwelling units and potentially the level of inmigration to a community due to expanding employment opportunities. And higher per capita personal income resulting from expanded employment opportunities increases demand for housing. (Although income is not treated separately in this report, its relationship to employment, housing demand, and property value is noted.)

While this report offers no explicit judgment on the relative impact of land development on each of these three areas of the economy, employment is treated in the greatest detail. The major emphasis on employment here reflects both the limited published information available elsewhere and the strong interest in the subject, as expressed by local officials. Housing is also emphasized, reflecting the desire of local officials to estimate the effects of new residential development on housing needs of the community. Changes in property value are treated more briefly than employment or housing. This reflects both the scarcity of analysis on this subject and the limitations of the tools used to estimate the effects of new development.

The cited study of fiscal impact shows that, from the community perspective, specific developments may have positive or negative fiscal effects. Although increases in employment and housing can have some negative impact, expanded employment and housing opportunities have positive aggregate effects on both the private and public sectors. Because changes in property value have distributional effects, some segments of the population will benefit from increases in property value while others will not benefit, at least not in the short run.

The economic effects of new development should take both environmental and social impacts into consideration if a balanced evaluation is to be produced. Since these areas are the subjects of other reports in this series, their effects are not considered in this report.[2]

In addition to local concerns, a number of states, such as Florida and Montana, presently require that employment effects be examined as part of state-mandated impact evaluation.[3] The impact of development on housing is also assessed as part of the Florida Development of Regional Impact (DRI) process. Changes in property value, if they have a growth-inducing effect, are part of the Environmental Impact Reports (EIRs) in California and other states. These reports should provide some assistance to staffs undertaking or evaluating the nonfiscal economic effects of development.

The two main topics of the report, employment and housing, are also key elements in most land use models. Input for these models is the location of goods-producing (export) industries. The demand for housing is derived from two sources: the household location of employees in goods-producing industries, and income. Population-serving industries, such as retail outlets and personal services, are assigned to specific locations as a function of the regional distribution of the population. (The change in the selling price of unimproved land and improvements, the third topic of this report, is not included in most land use models.)

---

2. Dale Keyes, Land Development and the Natural Environment: Estimating Impacts, (Washington, D.C.: The Urban Institute, February 1976); Kathleen Christensen, Estimating the Social Impacts of Land Development (Washington, D.C.: The Urban Institute, forthcoming).

3. For an assessment of the quality of economic impact reports in several states, see Thomas Muller and Kathleen Christensen, State Mandated Impact Evaluation (Washington, D.C.: The Urban Institute, June 1976).

Figure 1 illustrates the sequence for the report. Part I discusses methods for estimating employment by type and income, and the household location of employees. A major source of demand for new housing units discussed in Part II is derived from expanded employment opportunities. The subject of Part III, the demand for land and its value, is influenced by the location of both new nonresidential development and housing built to accommodate new employees.

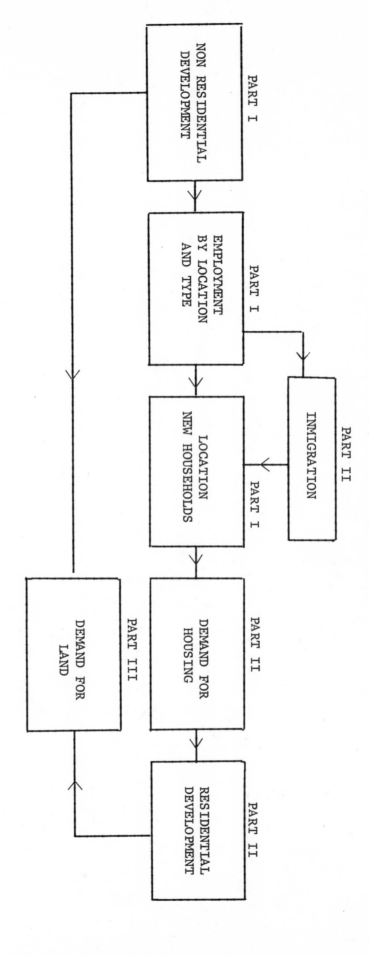

FIGURE 1. MAJOR COMPONENTS OF REPORT

PART I—IMPACT OF LAND DEVELOPMENT ON EMPLOYMENT

# I. INTRODUCTION AND BACKGROUND

Increased employment opportunities and the associated changes in personal income resulting from new development are the most important positive impacts of growth. Wages and salaries account for 75 percent of all personal income. Since new private employment is primarily the result of commercial and industrial development, the report focuses on these categories of growth. The impact of residential growth on construction and municipal jobs is also discussed. As indicated in the overview report on impact evaluation, two employment statistics are relevant in this context: (1) the number of new long- and short-term jobs provided by new development, including the share of jobs filled by current community residents, and (2) change in the employment and unemployment rates for the local work force.[1]

The introductory section of this chapter notes the relationship between employment and other measurements of impact. Objectives of employment impact analyses, as viewed from the local government perspective, are briefly considered. Subsequent chapters discuss methods for estimating changes in employment, unemployment, and the likely residence of newly employed workers. The discussion focuses on estimating local employment (although employment patterns tend to be regional).

---

1. Philip S. Schaenman, Using an Impact Measurement System to Evaluate Land Development (Washington, D.C.: The Urban Institute, 1976).

A. RELATIONSHIP BETWEEN EMPLOYMENT EFFECTS AND COMPREHENSIVE IMPACT EVALUATION

Employment is closely linked to other economic and noneconomic aspects of impact evaluation. These include fiscal, housing, wealth, and transportation considerations.

The fiscal impact of new development depends largely on the income of residents attracted to a community. This in turn is linked to the type of employment opportunities associated with the development. Demand for housing increases as new development expands employment opportunities and earnings. Thus, one measure of likely housing demand by type is the number and estimated income of projected employees. Areas of population growth, generally resulting from employment growth, produce more rapid increases in residential property values than areas with net outmigration. As a result of these and other linkages, employment impact must be viewed as part of a comprehensive impact evaluation.

B. OBJECTIVES OF EMPLOYMENT IMPACT ANALYSIS

Most local governments promote employment growth within their communities. Frequently, however, local officials must choose between new employment and the potentially adverse environmental and social effects of development. An employment impact analysis can assist in this choice by assessing how many new jobs, and at what income level, will be created if a new industrial or commercial development is approved; what share of new jobs is likely to be taken by community residents; how unemployment can be reduced; and what level, if any, of inmigration will take place. If a development has already been approved, an employment impact analysis can still be used in planning the location and size of public facilities, and in assessing the development's likely fiscal impact.

## C. EMPLOYMENT OBJECTIVES OF LOCAL JURISDICTIONS

Most local governments promote employment growth to achieve one or more of the following objectives:

1. <u>Reducing Unemployment and Underemployment</u>. Communities with substantial levels of unemployment or underemployment are anxious to reduce these levels for social, political, and economic reasons. The most direct way to accomplish this objective is to expand employment opportunities, particularly by attracting new industry that needs locally available skills.

Communities are also anxious to improve opportunities for unskilled, low salaried employees and for skilled workers who are unable to obtain appropriate work. Even jurisdictions with high household income and low unemployment rates are interested in expanding work opportunities for persons outside the work force such as students, the elderly, and women who can only work part time because of their children.

2. <u>Maintaining Overall Economic Viability and Stability</u>. Some jurisdictions consider new industry necessary to maintain the local private and public economy. As stated in the general plan for Howard County, Maryland, "for economic viability, a community needs an adequate (new) supply of enterprises affording job opportunities."[2] Although "viability" is not defined, it is implicit that a community requires new industry to increase personal income and the rate of local labor participation. New industry, in turn, will not only aid other business firms in the community but also provide goods and services. New job opportunities are also likely to reduce the outmigration of young persons who are entering the labor force.

---

2. Maryland, Howard County, <u>Howard County Plan</u> (1967).

3. <u>Improving Fiscal Structure</u>   It is generally assumed that new commercial and industrial facilities provide fiscal surpluses for the community since such facilities typically require less in services than they pay in property and other taxes.  Since few industries are fully automated, attracting new industry implies expanding employment opportunities.  New employees, even if not local residents, are likely to patronize local businesses. Therefore, sales tax and other revenues can be expected to increase as a result of employment expansion.

4. <u>Increasing Economic Stability</u>   The existence of a broad range of employment opportunities can mitigate the negative effect of an employment reduction by any one firm.  For example, if a community's largest employer is a military base, the closing of this facility would cause major economic dislocation unless alternative employment opportunities were available.

5. <u>Reducing Level of Congestion</u>   Suburban communities, such as Fairfax County in the Washington, D.C., SMSA, are typically eager to "intercept" some of the automobile traffic passing through them to the central city by expanding employment opportunities within their jurisdictions.  The average number of commuters can be reduced greatly if there is a greater balance between the total number of employed persons and the number of job opportunities within the community.

D.  <u>ORGANIZATION OF PART I</u>

The sequence of analysis to determine the impact of new development is shown in Figure 2.  Chapter II of Part I shows how to estimate the total level of short- and long-term employment associated with new development in the private and public sector.  Chapter III discusses factors that determine the share of total new employees likely to be local residents,

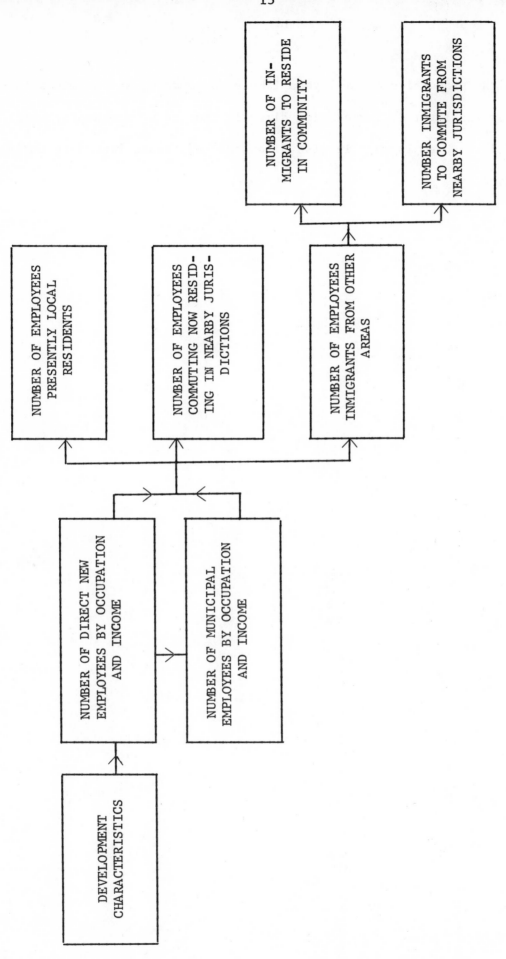

FIGURE 2. NEW LONG-TERM EMPLOYMENT GROUPED BY RESIDENCE

indicates the proportion of employees likely to commute, and examines factors that affect the level of inmigration directly induced by new employment opportunities. Unemployment is also discussed and issues linked to employment are noted.

## II. EMPLOYMENT EFFECTS OF LAND DEVELOPMENT

A. EMPLOYMENT CATEGORIES

1. Producers of Goods and Services. The national and local labor force is comprised both of those who are employed and unemployed, the latter defined as those seeking but unable to find work. New development can affect both groups.

Employment can be grouped into two major categories: goods-producing and service-producing jobs. The former include jobs in manufacturing, mining, construction, and agriculture. Most of the goods produced locally, except those for use in construction, are exported to other parts of the region or the nation. Service-producing jobs, such as those in trade, finance, transportation, utilities, and government, account for about 60 percent of total employment. Most services are provided in local or metropolitan markets. Exceptions include federal or state government employment, which serves a large geographic area. Large city corporate headquarters also export their services nationally.

New developments can create either goods-producing or service-producing jobs. Export-producing jobs are frequently defined as primary or basic, since funds obtained from the sale of goods outside the area pay the wages and salaries that enable employees to buy local goods and services. Commercial development generally creates service-producing jobs; whereas industrial development usually creates goods-producing employment. Wages in goods-producing jobs are considerably higher than wages in service industries.

2. <u>Short- and Long-Term</u>. Short-term jobs are those which are not permanent at one site. Typical are construction jobs which may last, at a specific site, from only a few weeks to one or two years. Construction workers' characteristics and impact on housing differ from those of other job categories.

The short-term employment discussed in this Chapter is almost exclusively in the construction sector. Excluded are seasonal jobs, such as at recreation facilities, in agriculture, and in some industries. Long-term jobs are those which are permanent or semipermanent at one site.

3. <u>Private and Public Sector</u>. While most jobs exist in the private sector, employment in local and state government is increasing more rapidly than is employment in the private sector. Generally, public jobs follow private employment. However, in areas such as Washington, D.C., or in state capitals, where public employment forms the major export industry, private jobs follow the expansion of the public sector. This report, however, discusses only public sector employment resulting from an expansion of private residential and nonresidential development.

4. <u>Primary and Second-Order</u>. The primary focus here is on estimating jobs linked directly to new industrial, commercial, or residential facilities. Second-order employment effects, with the exception of local public and construction sectors, are noted only briefly; additional jobs created by goods-producing or other primary economic activities are difficult to estimate at the local level.

B. <u>LAND USE FACTORS AFFECTING EMPLOYMENT</u>

1. <u>Background</u>. Both the type and level of employment differ substantially by type of land use--residential, commercial, industrial, or institutional. Correspondingly, wages of employees, and thus the economic effect of new

development, vary considerably. The impact of alternative developments on employment by type is shown in Table I-1. Average weekly wages by type of development and employment category are shown in Table I-2.

2. <u>Residential Development</u>. Such development in a community creates both short-term construction employment in the private and public sector and long-term public employment. While the <u>level</u> of short-term employment is not sensitive to the type of construction (such as highrise structures, townhouses, detached housing units) for equivalent dollar outlays, public employment can vary substantially as a result of the housing mix. For example, a highrise building with elderly tenants is unlikely to increase the demand for teachers. But it will increase the consumption of medical services. New detached housing units, in contrast, are likely to mean more school children and cause an increase in the demand for certain recreational facilities.

3. <u>Shopping Centers</u>. The construction of shopping centers requires short-term workers and also provides long-term private employment, mostly at low and moderate wage levels. New <u>office construction</u> can result in a variety of long-term jobs at various wage levels, primarily in the private sector.

4. <u>Industrial Development</u>. In addition to providing short-term construction work, new industrial facilities expand long-term jobs in the private sector. A large share of industrial jobs in urban areas involves manufacturing, where wages are generally above the average of those in other sectors except construction.

5. <u>Institutional Development</u>. This group of facilities usually include buildings such as schools, cultural centers, or stadiums, which serve government or quasipublic agencies. These facilities, which generally follow private employment, will be noted in the section discussing public employment. Average wages in the public sector exceed mean wages in the private sector.

Table I-1. IMPACT OF ALTERNATIVE DEVELOPMENTS ON EMPLOYMENT

| TYPE OF DEVELOPMENT | SHORT-TERM JOBS | | LONG-TERM JOBS | |
| --- | --- | --- | --- | --- |
| | Private Sector | Public Sector | Private Sector | Public Sector |
| Residential Housing | S | M-S | N | S |
| Shopping Center | S | M | S | M-N |
| Office | S | M | S | M-N |
| Industrial | S | M | S | M-N |
| Institutional | M-N | M-N | M-N | S |

S = Substantial Impact.
M = Moderate Impact.
N = No or Minor Impact.

Table I-2. AVERAGE WEEKLY WAGES FOR SELECTED EMPLOYMENT CATEGORIES
DURING 1973

| EMPLOYMENT CATEGORY | TYPE OF DEVELOPMENT | AVERAGE WEEKLY WAGE[a] |
|---|---|---|
| Short-Term Private | | |
|     Construction | All | $241 |
| Long-Term Private | | |
|     Wholesale and Retail Trade | Commercial | $111 |
|     Finance, Insurance, Real Estate | Commercial | $134 |
|     Manufacturing | Industrial | $166 |
|     Services | Commercial | $115 |
| Total Private | All | $144 |
| Long-Term Public | | |
|     Municipal Services | Institutional | $162 |
| Total Public (local, state, federal) | All | $180 |

Source: U.S., Department of Labor, 1974 Handbook of Labor Statistics, bulletin
1825, Washington, D.C., 1975.

a/ Based on monthly wages earned during April 1973.

C.  SHORT-TERM PRIVATE SECTOR EMPLOYMENT

1.  Background.  New developments create short-term private sector employment, primarily in the high wage construction trades.  Most of the jobs created involve the preparation of sites and construction of residential, commercial, industrial, or institutional facilities.  Additional workers are required to construct part of the infrastructure within and in some cases outside the development's boundaries, including internal streets, water and sewer lines, and drainage pipes.  Telephone and electrical lines are placed by local utility companies.  Some white collar workers, such as engineers, architects, and planners, are also employed before and during construction.

The number of employees (or person-years of employment) can be estimated directly from records maintained by construction companies, or indirectly from data on the cost of construction.  Wages can also be estimated directly from records or based on regional averages.

2.  Data Collection and Analysis.  Available data on private construction cost for single-family housing show that a typical house (1,622 square feet) requires 1,337 hours of on-site labor.[1]  An additional 1,925 industry person-hours are required off-site to produce construction material, and 254 off-site person-hours are needed in contractor's offices.  Total employment for a detached house is thus about 0.65 person-year on-site and about one person-year off-site.

By comparison, 638 person-hours of on-site labor were required in 1971 to construct an average apartment.[2]  On a per-square-foot basis, 65 on-site construction hours were required in 1970 to build 100 square feet of

---

1.  U.S., Department of Labor, Labor and Material Required for Construction of Private Single-Family Houses, bulletin 1755 (1972).

2.  Robert Ball, "Labor and Material Requirements for Apartment Construction," Monthly Labor Review (January 1975).  Per $1,000 of construction outlay, the number of construction hours required to build single-family and multiple unit structures is the same.

apartment floor area. Thus, the "average" apartment which requires 638 hours has 982 square feet of floor area.

On-site wages, based on U.S. Department of Labor studies, represent about 25 percent of the cost of private single or multiple unit structures but account for 35 percent of public housing cost. The differences in the wage factor in private and public housing may be due, in part, to higher wages paid to construction workers in projects involving public funds, since union labor must be used in federally-funded construction projects.

A 1967 study of housing indicates that on-site labor represents 41 percent of the cost of walk-up apartments and 42 percent of the cost of highrise apartments sponsored by HUD.[3] The high percentage of labor cost in this study may be attributable to the location of the apartments used to derive estimates. These apartments were located in the Northeast, where construction wages are typically higher than for other regions.[4]

An additional source of information for employment data is the state of Florida, where legislation requires that developers provide data on the labor share of total construction cost as well as on the number of construction workers to be employed in large-scale projects. An examination of several predominantly residential Development of Regional Impact (DRI) applications indicates that on-site construction wages are expected to account for 37 to 41 percent of total construction outlays.

It is possible to estimate total person-hours (person-years) of construction labor if average hourly construction wages and total project costs are known. Table I-3 demonstrates such an estimation.

3. Elsa Eaves, How the Many Costs of Housing Fit Together (Washington, D.C.: National Committee on Urban Relations, 1969).
4. The methodology used in the study differs somewhat from that in the Department of Labor analyses, contributing to differences in the share of labor costs.

Table I-3.  CONVERSION OF PROJECT COST TO CONSTRUCTION LABOR TIME

Total Project Cost                                              $7,000,000

Estimated Labor Share of Total Construction Cost                    32%

Average Area Wage Per Hour[a/]                                     $9.00

Number of Housing Units Constructed                                 170

Number of Construction Person-Years $= \dfrac{\$7,000,000 \times 0.32}{\$9.00 \times 2,000 \;\underline{a/}} = \dfrac{2,240,000}{18,000} = 124$

Number of Person-Years Per Housing Unit $= 0.73$

------------------------------------------------------------------

a/  40 Hours x 50 Weeks.

Data on average construction wages for selected areas can be obtained from the Department of Labor's Bureau of Labor Statistics.  More detailed data comparing differences in labor costs by areas, updated annually, are available from a private source.[5]  This publication, for example, indicates that the average urban wage per hour (including benefits) in construction during 1974 was $10.00.  However, there was substantial nationwide variation, from $7.60 in Austin, Texas, to $12.30 in New York City.

Since there are regional and other differences in employment created by new construction, local governments should obtain wage data including the ratio of on-site wages to contract value for typical projects directly from local contractors' associations.  In the absence of such local wage data, the method illustrated in Table I-3 should provide a reasonable substitute.  Since most off-site jobs are located away from the area where the development takes place, wage data should not be estimated for this category.

------------------------------------------------------------------

5.  Dodge Manual for Building Construction (New York: McGraw-Hill Systems, 1974).

D.  SHORT-TERM PUBLIC SECTOR EMPLOYMENT

1.  Background.  In many instances, new residential development will require the expansion of public facilities to meet the needs of new residents. Such expansion may include extending the road network, building new schools and fire stations, adding to existing structures, or constructing other facilities typically provided by local government.  The likelihood of an immediate expansion depends on such factors as the size of new development, the utilization rate of facilities already in place, and the availability of public funds.  In some communities, such as those with five- or ten-year capital improvement programs, the infrastructure may include a planned overcapacity in anticipation of future development in specified locations.  In other cases, outmigration, or demographic changes such as smaller households, may have reduced the demand for classrooms and other facilities, resulting in an underutilized infrastructure.  Because of the "lumpy" nature of the data about some facilities such as schools and sewage treatment plants, a single development may not trigger the need for addition or expansion of facilities.  However, in most cases, large residential developments will require some additional public capital investment, particularly in road construction.[6]

Nonresidential development, such as a shopping center, is most likely to require an expansion of roads and utilities.  Facilities which provide educational, social, and recreational services are not directly affected by new commercial and industrial development.

2.  Data Collection and Analysis.  The suggested method for estimating employment resulting from the expansion of public facilities is that used for privately sponsored development--converting the cost of expansion into its major components, direct on-site labor, material, and overhead.  While public outlays

_____

6.  The necessity for additional investment triggered by new development is least likely in large central cities with declining populations, most likely in rapidly growing suburban and exurban areas.

are financed by taxes or fees, construction is usually performed by private contractors. The one notable difference between a privately and publicly sponsored project is the cost of labor, which tends to be higher for publicly funded construction.[7]

The initial step in estimating employment impact is to determine whether existing facilities can absorb the additional demand created by the new development. If capacity is insufficient, the community must choose between service degradation (road congestion, overcrowded schools, partially treated sewage) or the expansion of facilities.

Data on the cost of expanding facilities should be based on recent experiences of the community or nearby jurisdictions. Since the cost of labor or material will vary only slightly within a metropolitan area, costs can be estimated from contracts for similar facilities. In the absence of local data, an excellent source for estimating the cost of public buildings by urban area is the McGraw-Hill construction publication series.[8] Once the cost of expanding facilities is known, the labor share and person-hours of labor can be estimated by using the procedures discussed in the "Short-Term Private Sector Employment" section of this report.

The largest nonbuilding public outlay associated with new development is road construction. The on-site labor share of the total contract value of such construction is estimated at 25 percent, and the cost of material at 45 percent. Overhead items such as off-site salaries, equipment, and profit account for the balance, or 30 percent.[9] While specific data are unavailable for utilities, the on-site labor share probably approximates that shown for highway construction.

---

7. There may be other differences, such as meeting federal or state facility standards, which can increase construction costs.

8. For example, see Dodge Building Cost and Specification Digest (New York: McGraw-Hill Systems, 1973). This publication contains aggregate and per-square-foot costs, updated annually.

9. U.S., Department of Labor, "Labor and Material Required for Highway Construction," Monthly Labor Review (June 1973).

E.  LONG-TERM PRIVATE EMPLOYMENT

1.  Background.  A major objective of most local governments is to increase private sector employment opportunities for residents.  Since construction workers usually account for only 4 to 8 percent of the total local work force, most governments attempt to provide long-term employment opportunities.  Most direct long-term private employment is the result of commercial and industrial development.[10]  This section discusses various methods to estimate the level of employment and wages.

2.  Data Collection and Analysis.  Commercial employment includes two major categories: employment in retail stores such as in shopping centers, and office employment.  Since shopping center construction data are usually available in terms of square feet of space, related employment figures can be derived using employee-per-square-foot ratios.  Such ratios will differ by type of retail establishment and location.  For example, a self-service drug or department store will employ fewer persons per square foot than will a "full service" department store.  There may also be some scale economies in large stores, such as supermarkets, which generally employ fewer persons per square foot than do small neighborhood convenience goods stores.  Data by two-digit industry groupings on the number of square feet of land per employee are available in a report prepared for the Federal Highway Administration.[11]  These data are based on national patterns.

A second approach is to use projected sales from new retail outlets.  Data on sales per square foot by type of retail outlet in shopping centers, updated

---

10.  Some direct long-term private employment also expands as a result of residential housing.  For example, apartments usually require managers and maintenance crews.

11.  Estimating Land and Floor Area Implicit in Employment Projections (Philadelphia: IDE Associates, July 1972).

every two or three years, are available from the Urban Land Institute.[12] For

example, in 1974 the median figure for sales per square foot in supermarkets

was $113; in furniture stores, $90; and in paint and wallpaper stores, $50.

The highest figure for sales per square foot, $125, was in fast-food carryouts.

These data can be converted to number of employees, by SMSA or state, by using

Bureau of the Census information on retail trades.[13] This information shows

the number of employees and their wages by retail store category. The follow-

ing tabulation provides an example of such a conversion.

Example: a furniture store with 15,000 square feet of space will be part

of the projected shopping center in Amarillo, Texas. How many employees, at

what wages, can be anticipated?

(1)  Number of Square Feet:  15,000 (given by developer).

(2)  Sales per Square Foot (1974):  $90.[14]

(3)  Projected Sales: (1) x (2): $1,350,000.

(4)  Number of Employees per $1 million in Sales, Amarillo, 1972: 16.[15]

(5)  Number of Projected Employees:  24 (from (3) and (4)).

(6)  Wages as Percent of Sales, 1972:  15%.[16]

(7)  Anticipated Aggregate Wages:  $202,500 (6 x 3).

(8)  Average Wage per Employee:  $8,437 (7÷5).

The Census of Retail Trades is published at five-year intervals. Annual

data on wages and wages as a percentage of retail sales are also available from

---

12.  Dollars and Cents of Shopping Centers-1975 (Washington, D.C.: Urban Land Institute, 1975).

13.  U.S., Bureau of the Census, "Major Retail Centers in SMSAs," 1972 Census of Retail Trades (Washington, D.C.: April 1975). Data refer to all retail stores, both old and new. Newer retail stores are larger and have fewer employees per square foot compared with those built in the past. (Between 1972 and 1974, inflation probably reduced the number of employees per dollar of sales by 10 to 15 percent).

14. ULI, Dollars and Cents of Shopping Centers.

15. Census, Major Retail Centers in SMSAs.

16. Ibid.

an annual publication of the Bureau of the Census.[17] The lag between the year of the survey and date of publication is about two years. This latter source indicates, for example, that the payroll in "eating and drinking places" in California is 25 percent of gross sales; in convenience retail stores, the payroll is only 13 percent of retail sales. The method of estimating which was used in a study of San Francisco highrise development and other reports, is more reliable than estimating employment based on square feet of space independent of tenant characteristics.[18]

A third, direct method of estimating employment for a particular development is to obtain a list of merchants who have leased space in the development, and to contact these merchants or store managers to determine their anticipated employment levels. A limitation of this method is the fact that frequently the developer may only have leased a small percentage of space at the time the request for rezoning or construction is filed.

Some states require developers to submit employment information. A fourth method consists of examination of this information. One such application, a DRI in Leon County, Florida, estimates 1,200 employees for a shopping center with 900,000 square feet of commercial space and an annual payroll of $7.4 million, or wages of about $6,200 per employee.[19]

To determine how close this estimate of employment approximates that for other shopping centers in the Southeast, Census of Retail Trades statistics are compared with the Florida data, as shown in the following tabulation:

---

17. U.S., Bureau of the Census, County Business Patterns, annual reports by state.
18. San Francisco Planning and Urban Renewal Association, Impact of Intensive High Rise Development in San Francisco, preliminary draft (October 1974).
19. Capital Circle Mall, Leon County, Florida, Application for Employment Approval, Major Realty Company (Report filed with State of Florida, Tallahassee, dated January 1974).

(1) Sales per square foot--Southeast U.S. Regional
shopping centers a/                                                $68

(2) Number of square feet [b]                                       900,000

(3) Estimated sales (1 x 2) [b]                                     $61.2 million

(4) Estimated annual payroll [b]                                    7.4 million

(5) Annual payroll as a percent of sales (3) ÷ (4)                 12%

(6) Annual payroll as a percent of sales, Florida SMSA
retail centers c/                                                 12%

---

a/ Dollars and Cents of Shopping Centers-1975, (Washington, D.C.: Urban Land
Institute, 1975).
b/ From DRI Application.
c/ U.S., Bureau of the Census, Census of Retail Trades-Florida, 1975.

Annual payroll as a percent of sales estimated by both techniques is the same.

Differences in the payroll share shown in an application or questionnaires and

that shown in Census data do not necessarily indicate that the estimates are

incorrect. However, a major deviation indicates that further discussion should

be held with applicants to determine why submitted data vary from the usual

regional patterns.

Long-term retail sales employment can be generated by added residential

development independent of additional construction activity. For example, more

sales and other personnel will be required if the volume of sales in existing

retail establishments rises substantially as a result of additional purchasing

power by new residents. However, increases without physical expansion may be

only short run. Presumably, the expanded volume of sales would result in the

construction of new facilities by competitors or the expansion of existing

establishments. Therefore, an increase in sales employment can be anticipated

if sizable new residential developments are approved. In some cases, shopping

centers are built with overcapacity in anticipation of additional adjacent

housing. In this situation, retail employment would also increase.

3.  Office Employment. Wages in retail trades, as shown in Table I-2, account for only 57 percent of wages in manufacturing. Thus, the economic impact of expanded job opportunities is substantially less in this sector than if industrial jobs expand. However, since many retail sales jobs are "secondary," these jobs increase aggregate household income.

The office labor force includes workers in finance, insurance, real estate, professional services (physicians, consultants, attorneys) and related fields. Thus, wages and salaries will vary greatly within this category. The number of potential employees as a result of new office buildings can be estimated by one or more of the following techniques:

1.  Estimate employment from the overall national average ratio of eight workers per 1,000 square feet of net office space.

2.  Obtain direct data from managers leasing new office space.

3.  Survey existing office buildings in the community.

Data on the relationship between sales volume for selected services, number of workers, and annual wages can be determined from Census publications.[20] Thus, employment can be estimated if the volume of anticipated sales is known.

Both shopping center and office workers are typically involved in service employment--providing goods and services for those engaged in primary or basic employment activities. The income of office workers usually will be much higher than the income of persons employed in shopping centers.

4.  Industrial Employment. Most local governments prefer to attract industrial rather than commercial development. In part, this reflects the knowledge that most commercial facilities will follow residential development.

---

20. U.S., Bureau of the Census, 1972 Census of Selected Service Industries (Washington, D.C.: 1974). Data on services are available for SMSAs in each state.

Equally important, industrial wages, particularly in manufacturing, are substantially higher than are wages in commercial facilities. As was shown in
Table I-2. the average weekly wage in manufacturing is 77 percent higher than
in retail sales and 47 percent higher than in services. Industry, however, can
be selective in its choice of a site, particularly within an urbanized area.
Such factors as accessibility to transportation facilities, availability of
land, and tax rates are included in the location decision.

Unlike most commercial development, industrial employment levels cannot
be reliably estimated by facility size since employment levels vary greatly
within the industrial sector, and since the particular type of industry that
will locate in an industrial park may not be known at the time of a land use
decision. For example, capital-intensive industries such as chemical processing and most utilities employ relatively few people. Labor-intensive industries,
such as the textile industry, tend to have a high employee-to-square-foot
ratio. One general guide is to estimate the number of workers based on capital
investment per employee by industry. If a particular industry requires $100,000
in capital outlay per worker, a $5 million facility will employ roughly 50
workers. Data on capital investment per worker are available from the U. S.
Bureau of the Census.[21] However, technological changes and variations in product
mix can cause wide fluctuations among similar facilities.

An alternative approach is to apply data on the number of employees per
acre for two-digit industries based on national average.[22]

---

21. U.S., Bureau of the Census, Census of Manufacturing, issued every
five years.

22. For one source of these data, see Decision Sciences Corporation,
Advanced New Community Simulation System-Industrial Demand Model (Jenkintown,
Pa.: 1973).

A direct method for estimating level of employment is to obtain data from the builders of a facility. In most cases, industrial facilities are built in accordance with the needs of a particular business firm rather than in anticipation of potential tenants. In those cases involving speculative building (for example, warehouses, which require only minimal modification for various uses), industrywide ratios of employment per square foot can be applied.

Wage data are necessary to estimate the fiscal impact of development and to estimate the effects of growth in the private economy. Information on average wages paid by industry at the county level can also be obtained from the U.S. Bureau of the Census.[23] To derive average annual wages, multiply the quarterly payrolls listed in the publication by four. The resulting payroll figure is then divided by the number of employees in the industry.

Other sources for wage information include the U.S. Department of Labor, which publishes data on hourly wages in selected cities for many occupations, trade associations, and data from the 1970 census of population. The latter lists median earning for all industries, by sex and race. For example, full-time workers in the "office, accounting and computing machinery" sector earned an average of $11,226 in 1969, while those in "yarn, thread and fabric mills" earned only $6,096.[24] The Department of Labor also publishes data on the proportion of professional workers by industry. In petroleum refining, for example, it is estimated that 28 percent of the total work force in the late 1970s will be professional workers, compared to 50 percent of the total work force in plastic products.[25] Such data, in the absence of statistics

---

23. U.S., Bureau of the Census, County Business Patterns.
24. U.S., Bureau of the Census, 1970 Census of Population Supplementary Report, PC (SI)-44, June 1973. These data are, however, now obsolete.
25. U.S., Department of Labor, Tomorrow's Manpower Needs, vol. IV, bulletin 1606 (February 1969).

about occupants of the future facilities, can provide substantial information on likely characteristics of employees, such as their occupation mix and wage levels. Annual wage data are also available for manufacturing industries in large cities and in all counties in the nation.[26]

## F. LONG-TERM PUBLIC SECTOR EMPLOYMENT

1. Background. Public employment providing local services has increased sharply during the last three decades. Wages in the public sector since the mid-1960s have exceeded the private sector average (see Table I-2). At the end of 1973, local government nationally employed 8.4 million persons, representing 11.5 percent of the total nonagricultural work force and 4 percent of the population. Thus, for every 1,000 persons working, 115 are employed directly by local government. However, the proportion of municipal workers varies substantially among communities. Because more than 60 percent of all local government workers are associated with the public school systems, in-migration of households with a large number of school-age children is likely to increase the local public sector work force considerably more than a development of similar size which attracts primarily childless households.

2. Data Collection and Analysis. The relationship between residential development and increased demand for public services has been discussed in a previous Urban Institute publication in this series.[27] Local governments frequently apply employee-to-population ratios to estimate the effect of new development on municipal workers. For example, if a community school system

---

26. See Census, Census of Manufacturing, issued every five years and Survey of Manufacturing, issued annually.
27. Thomas Muller, Fiscal Impact of Land Development: A Critique of Methods and Review of Issues (Washington, D.C.: The Urban Institute, 1975).

employs one professional teacher or administrator per 20 students and one nonprofessional employee per 80 students, an increase of 320 students would require
an additional 16 teachers and four nonprofessional workers. Similarly, a
community standard of two police officers per 1,000 residents would expand the
police force by three.

In a school system with diminishing enrollment, the addition of students
from new developments may stabilize rather than increase employment. However,
if additional teachers are needed as a result of a new development, they should
be considered as part of increased employment (or, more precisely, prevented
unemployment) due to development, although the absolute number of teachers
remains the same.

In addition to teachers, other staffs associated with the school system
and the departments of public safety, parks, recreation, sanitation, and
libraries will experience employment increases as a result of new residential
development.

The number of municipal employees per capita increases as the size of the
jurisdiction expands.[28] The following should be considered when projecting
public employment from historical data:

1.  Public employment has been growing nationally at a faster rate than
    population growth. Communities with growing populations have fewer
    municipal workers per capita compared to cities with declining popu-
    lations, while large cities have more workers per capita than smaller
    jurisdictions.[29]

2.  In the short run, expansion of public employment is likely to be a
    function of budget flexibility rather than the change in the demand
    for services. However, public employment can be expected to increase,
    over time, at a level at least equal to population growth linked to
    development.

28. See U.S., Bureau of the Census, 1972 Census of Governments (Washington,
D.C.: Government Printing Office, 1973) for data on the number of municipal workers per capita for major functions and wages for municipal workers. Once a city
reaches a population of 50,000 or so, scale economies for most services are no
longer common. However, declining cities have scale diseconomies.

29. See Thomas Muller, Growing and Declining Urban Areas: A Fiscal Comparison (Washington, D.C.: The Urban Insitute, 1975) for a discussion of
factors causing these differences.

Commercial and industrial development is most likely to increase public employment in the areas of public safety and transportation, since these services are used in nonresidential activities. There are currently no reliable techniques for estimating the level of additional public employment for services jointly used by residential and nonresidential developments. However, a large number of new workers concentrated in one industrial facility will probably require more traffic control. Similarly, a large number of consumers in a shopping center will require additional foot patrols as well as traffic control measures.[30] One way to estimate the number of workers in an area dominated by commercial facilities is to compare the demand for services between predominantly commercial and residential areas. For example, the city of San Francisco's Central Business District (CBD) accounts for 24 percent of all police calls and 22 percent of all fire calls in the city, although only 11 percent of city residents live there. The demand for services and the number of municipal personnel assigned to that area, on a per capita basis, are roughly double the levels in predominantly residential areas. The daytime CBD population, roughly three times the resident population, presumably accounts for the higher level of service demand.

Nonmunicipal public employment will also expand as a result of new private development. Additional state employment is likely to be concentrated in hospitals, higher education, and other social services. Federal employment most directly related to new development is in the postal service. In a typical urban area, there is one state employee for every four municipal workers, and about three post office workers per 1,000 residents. Thus, state employment must be considered in any evaluation of a large development.

---

30. Nonresidential development does not create a _direct_ demand for schools, social services, or recreation. Frequently, industry provides private substitutes for public services. Many shopping centers employ private police and fire personnel.

If a community has not established guidelines or estimates linking new population with increased local public employment, a retrospective analysis can be undertaken to identify the service demand and manpower requirements associated with prior developments which are similar to the proposed development. Discussions with local planners and line agencies can also provide information concerning the possible need for new municipal workers. The following sequence of study tasks is appropriate:

1.  Estimate additional demand for services such as schools and public safety based on characteristics of new residents or industry.[31] It can be assumed, in the absence of contrary information, that the community will maintain existing service levels. Convert demand into public employee person-years.[32]

2.  Determine whether services are currently underutilized, i.e., can additional demand be absorbed without changing employment levels.

3.  Estimate additional persons who need to be hired (or who, in the absence of the new development, would lose their jobs), taking into account service underutilization, if any. If current budget limitations result in a postponement of hiring new persons, note likely time employment will be increased.

4.  Estimate numbers of professional and nonprofessional employment (or wage categories) based on current proportions.

---

31.  See Thomas Muller and Grace Dawson, _The Fiscal Impact of Residential and Commercial Development--A Case Study_ (Washington, D.C.: The Urban Institute, 1973) for an example of this process.

32.  Cross-sectional data show that large central cities have about ten municipal workers for functions other than education and hospitals for each 1,000 residents, inner suburbs, about six workers, and outer suburbs, about five workers. For additional statistics, see Muller, _Growing and Declining Urban Areas_.

# III. ESTIMATING THE PROPORTION OF NEW JOBS TAKEN BY COMMUNITY RESIDENTS

The previous section discussed methods to estimate the level, or quantity, of short- and long-term employment resulting from new residential and non-residential development. However, from the local government (rather than the regional) perspective, such aggregate numbers may be of only limited value. Most communities are concerned about increasing employment opportunities for their own residents rather than for future residents or for those residing in nearby communities. From a fiscal perspective, however, communities can frequently benefit by obtaining tax revenues from new industrial and commercial facilities and discouraging inmigration, particularly for lower wage jobs, which would expand demand for local services.

Estimating the total level of employment is only the first step in projecting the impact of new development on the local work force. The proportion of commuters and inmigrants filling newly created jobs must also be estimated. This kind of estimate is more difficult than projecting the aggregate level of employment which excludes considering the likely residence of new work force.

To begin the estimate, the employment status of the existing local labor pool should be examined to estimate the probable proportion of workers likely to be drawn from present residents of a community. Factors such as the composition of the labor force which affect the number of noncommunity residents likely to fill jobs are discussed in this section.

A.  RESIDENTS GROUPED BY CURRENT EMPLOYMENT STATUS

A major factor which determines the share of local residents filling new jobs is the proportion of the local labor pool that is presently employed, underemployed, unemployed, or no longer looking for work.

1. Workers Presently Fully Employed.  Most new jobs, particularly those requiring substantial skill and training, are taken by workers who transfer to a new facility for higher wages, better working conditions, improved accessibility to place of employment, or anticipated stability of the new firm.  (This assumes an overall low rate of unemployment in the region.)  The transfer, in turn, leaves an opening at the workers' previous place of employment for those with similar training.  If the transferring worker is a local resident and the position vacated is filled by a local resident, the net effect is a gain of one local job.  If the vacated job is taken by a commuter, the net employment effect on the community is zero.

2. Workers Presently Underemployed.  Underemployed workers are those employed on a part-time basis, although willing to work full time, or those working at jobs substantially below their ability because employment commensurate with their background is unavailable.  The likelihood that such workers will take new jobs depends primarily on the "match" between their abilities and the skill needs of the new development.

3. Workers Presently Unemployed.  Persons not working but actively seeking employment represent a group receiving special government attention.  It is unlikely that unemployed workers will be actively recruited outside the region, unless they possess particular skills and background not available in the region.

4. Persons Not in Labor Force.  Persons not part of the labor force but willing to work include teenagers seeking part-time work, housewives seeking full-time or part-time work, students completing their education, and the

semiretired seeking part-time work. With the exception of students completing their education, most potential workers in this group are residents of the region. Many in this group are likely to be "secondary" workers (in contrast to the head of the household who is usually the "primary" worker).

## B. VARIABLES AFFECTING RESIDENCE OF WORKERS

Potential workers live in the community where a new development is located or in nearby communities (the labor market area). In some cases they in-migrate to the labor market area in response to the new employment opportuni-ties. The proportions of workers likely to be community residents and commuters are functions of the following kinds of variables.

1. Types and Size of the Community. Three types of communities should be identified: central cities; suburbs of central cities; and smaller, non-metropolitan jurisdictions. Office employment tends to account for an increas-ing share of central city employment, as industrial facilities move from core locations to suburban and exurban areas. A study of office building employ-ment in the San Francisco CBD based on a questionnaire provides data on the characteristics of office workers.[33] It shows that a majority of higher wage employees, including 63 percent of managers and proprietors working in the business district, commute from the suburbs. Some 54 percent of the lower wage clerical workers reside in the city. More than 50 percent of females, who represent a large share of clerical employment, reside in the city, com-pared to 25 percent of males who live within the municipal boundaries. This is consistent with the pattern identified in other studies. About half of all workers 35 years of age and under live in the city, but two-thirds of older

33. Impact of Intensive, High Rise Development in San Francisco.

persons commute from other communities. As income increases, so does the likelihood of commuting to the central city. The pattern for San Francisco is similar to that drawn from census data wherein a high proportion of affluent household heads commute to central cities.[34] Additional office jobs created by commercial development in the central city are likely to attract city residents who are young females, with moderate incomes.

Suburban commercial development, such as shopping centers, is more likely to attract nearby workers rather than commuters from the central city. The likelihood of providing a substantial share of employment to residents of the community where the new development is located is also a function of the size of that suburb compared with other suburbs. Usually, one suburban community includes only a small part of the metropolitan labor force. In that case, a major share of workers will be residents of other suburbs and of the central city.

Small nonmetropolitan communities, which include a large proportion of the area labor force, are most likely to provide employment for their residents. In the absence of inmigration or long-distance commuting, employers must select workers from the existing labor pool concentrated in one community.

2. <u>Location of Development Within the Community</u>. A facility located near the boundary of another community is more likely to attract workers from the nearby community than a facility located in the center of a large jurisdiction. This pattern has been shown in at least one transportation study. The

------

34. While per capita income and wages of households residing in central cities of most Northeastern and North Central states tend to be below the suburban average, aggregate central city wages exceed the suburban level. This is attributable to higher wages of suburban commuters employed in cities.

transportation network between the development and nearby communities determines the length of the commuting time. This, in turn, influences the areas
from which workers are drawn. The driving time from origin to destination is
more important than the highway distance between the two points. The Northern
Virginia Transportation study found that only 36 percent of the employees of
a research facility close to the boundaries of a nearby county were county
residents, while 57 percent of the labor force of a similar facility closer
to the geographic center of the county were county residents. The same
study also shows that the addition of new expressways increases the geographic
area employees are likely to reside in by reducing the commuting time to
fringe areas.[35]

3. <u>Skill Level and Wage Structure</u>. A number of studies, including those
cited previously, show that jobs paying higher wages tend to attract workers
from a greater geographic area than do lower paying jobs.[36] Several factors
may explain this pattern:

1. To attract workers from some distance, one must pay high wages to
   offset the transportation cost of commuting;

2. Higher income households are (or can afford to be) more concerned
   with neighborhood amenities and the quality of local public services
   than transportation costs. More favorable living conditions may be
   found only at considerable distance from employment centers.[37] (Central
   city employment centers are frequently in areas of older, poorly maintained housing, with lower income residents).

---

35. <u>The Socio-Economic Impact of the Capital Beltway on Northern Virginia</u>,
appendix F-4 (Charlottesville: University of Virginia, 1969).

36. Robert J. Johnson, <u>Urban Residential Patterns</u> (New York: Praeger
Publishers, 1972).

37. Increasingly, however, regional shopping centers also attract office
complexes to nearby locations.

3. Higher income workers are more likely to have private automobiles and thus greater mobility to commute from greater distances.

Commuting patterns imply that, other factors held constant, a lower share of all available jobs will be filled by community residents if wages in new facilities are high, since potential community workers will be competing for new jobs with nonresidents willing to commute.

4. <u>Characteristics of the Community Labor Force</u>. The match between the existing labor and new job openings is the must important factor in determining whether local residents will seek employment in a new facility. In an affluent suburb comprised primarily of professional workers, the likelihood of a local resident taking a blue collar job may be small. However, if a new firm offers professional employment at comparable salary levels, many community residents who commute to the central city may apply for jobs.

5. <u>Previous Location of Facility</u>. If a facility relocates from one site to another within the metropolitan region, relatively few workers are likely [38] to change their current residence. Most workers will choose to commute to the new facility rather than to change jobs or place of residence within the region. Higher wage employees are more likely to keep their jobs and residences, even if commuting distance is increased than are those holding lower paying jobs. This means that the number of new job openings for local residents is likely to be limited, particularly for professional workers, if a facility relocates within the same region.

6. <u>Duration of Work (Short- or Long-Term)</u>. The proportion of on-site construction workers who are community residents varies widely among areas. Thus, many affluent suburban communities attract construction labor from nearby

---

38. See Louis K. Lowestein, "The Impact of New Industry on Revenue Expenditures of Suburban Communities," <u>National Tax Journal</u> (June 1963) for data on employee residence after relocation with the Philadelphia SMSA.

communities and rural areas. For example, it is not unusual in the Washington, D.C., SMSA to find many construction workers who commute from West Virginia and other locations 50 or more miles away. In Western states, construction workers frequently travel 100 miles or more to work. In predominantly blue collar jurisdictions, a large proportion of construction workers may be residents. Highly skilled workers in construction trades tend to migrate with job opportunities. The construction of the subway systems in the District of Columbia and in San Francisco has attracted subway construction specialists from many areas, and the Alaska pipeline has attracted welders from all regions of the nation. In general, construction workers, due to the short-term duration of their jobs at one location and high wages have a greater incidence of long-distance commuting than workers in other industries. Local contractors, union officials, and developers can be contacted to determine where most of their workers live.

The residence of long-term public employees can be estimated from municipal personnel records. In the District of Columbia, the majority of local workers, particularly in the police department, are not local residents. However, some communities give local residents job preference.

7. <u>Legal Requirements</u>. A number of jurisdictions, including Chicago and Detroit, <u>require</u> that municipal employees be residents of the city. If a community has such a requirement, presumably all municipal workers are, or will shortly become, city residents.

8. <u>Other Factors</u>. Other things being equal, local residents rather than those residing in other communities are more likely to take new jobs because of lower transportation costs, less commuting time, and greater access to information on the availability of new employment opportunities.

C.  METHODS TO CALCULATE SHARE OF EMPLOYMENT BY LOCATION

Most communities have little if any information on the residence of their
labor force beyond aggregate Census of Population data.  As a result, it is
difficult for jurisdictions to estimate the employment impact of new industrial
and commercial development on their residents.  Two general techniques are
suggested for developing such estimates: a retrospective examination of specific
industries within the community (micro-level data), and the use of aggregate
information based on previous studies.

1.  Direct Data from Local Industries.  A useful method for estimating
the type of employees likely to be local residents is to survey existing
industries within the community which are likely to expand.  Facilities which
have been located in the community for four or more years should be selected.
Personnel departments maintain data on the home residence of employees and
can provide information on occupation, income, and length of employment.  The
personnel department should also have data on the number of employees transferred or hired outside the region.[39]

A more extensive and therefore far more expensive effort includes questionnaires to be completed by employees.  A survey of employees in selected
industries should include the following information:

1.  Occupation,
2.  Jurisdiction of residence,
3.  Length of residence,
4.  Previous residences (by jurisdiction, state),
5.  Whether person inmigrated to region as a result of job agreement with
    present employer,
6.  Whether head of household or secondary worker,
7.  Education (highest level attained),
8.  Income,
9.  Sex,
10.  Previous occupation, and
11.  Previous work status (as unemployed, student).

_____

39.  Almost all organizations considered data, employee residence, and income to be confidential.  Thus, local agencies can obtain such data only by
agreeing that the data be kept so.

These data would provide a profile for use in evaluating the likely impact of new development on local employment.

2. Census Tract Information. The 1970 Census of Population and Housing provides data on workers by their place of residence at the census tract level for SMSAs. This information can be used to estimate the distance traveled from place of residence to place of employment. Since other census data on household characteristics, such as income and occupation, are also available, the characteristics of households most likely to commute to nearby jurisdictions can readily be ascertained. For example, a comparison of two adjacent census tracts in Loudoun County, Virginia, indicates that the proportion of residents commuting to other jurisdictions is considerably higher in the census tract having higher family incomes. In the case of the higher income census tract, more than 40 percent of those employed are professional workers or managers, while in the lower income tract, less than 10 percent are in this category. However, the census data estimates the number of residents working rather than the number of jobs in the census tract, and is limited in this respect.

3. Transportation Studies. Many large communities have undertaken transportation studies to establish trip generation patterns, generally based on travel between centers of employment and residential areas. The importance of such patterns for the location of new facilities and residential units has been noted in several analytic studies. The major limitation of transportation studies is that occupation and income data, necessary to assess the economic impact of new employment, are generally excluded from the data base.

4. Models of Employment and Residential Location. During the last two decades, a number of employment/residential location models have been developed.

Most have incorporated factors discussed in the previous sections. Among these efforts, the Kain model is perhaps the most interesting.[40] The central hypothesis of this model is that households substitute journey-to-work for site (housing) expenditures. That is, equivalent housing is less expensive as the distance from the urban employment center increases, while commuting costs rise, but less rapidly. Empirical data, based on information collected in Detroit, are presented to illustrate that the hypothesis is valid. Further, it is shown that larger families prefer to live further from the urban employment center, holding other factors constant. A major limitation of the study is that data were collected in 1953, when employment was concentrated in the central city. If the study were replicated in 1976, results would differ considerably.

As Lee notes, most land use models were initiated in the early 1960s, but largely abandoned by the end of the decade.[41] Major causes for the failure of large-scale models are discussed in Lee's somewhat harsh critique of modeling efforts. Communities considering the adaptation of large-scale land use models to estimate the employment and residential patterns are advised to read this article.

5. <u>Studies in Other Locations</u>. A study undertaken in New Jersey provides considerable insight into commuting patterns by industry.[42] One conclusion reached by this study is that manufacturing establishments attract workers from a more widespread area than do nonmanufacturing establishments. Reasons for this include higher wages and a higher proportion of male workers in the manufacturing sector. In the apparel industry, with mostly female employees,

---

40. John F. Kain, "The Journey-to-Work as a Determinant of Residential Location," <u>Papers and Proceedings of the Regional Science Association</u> (Philadelphia, Pa.: Regional Science Association, 1962).

41. Douglas B. Lee, Jr., "Requiem for Large-Scale Models," <u>Journal of the American Institute of Planners</u>, (May 1973).

42. New Jersey, Department of Labor and Industry, <u>Commuting Patterns of Workers Employed in New Jersey</u>, Research Series 3 (February 1961).

the commuting distance is typically very short. Those working in trade and
finance tend to work in the county of residence more than workers in other
nonmanufacturing sectors. While the data include only commuting patterns
within New Jersey, other, less comprehensive surveys point to the same conclu-
sions--that attracting a new industry to a community, particularly higher wage
industry or commerce, provides no assurance that persons taking new jobs will,
in fact, be community residents. The absence of housing and "desirable"
neighborhoods means that most higher wage workers will be commuters. Other
studies conclude that work place location does not significantly influence
resident location.[43] These studies indicate that most persons, particularly
those in high-income groups, are more concerned with neighborhood quality than
with accessibility as measured by distance to work.[44]

D. BASIC ANALYTICAL TECHNIQUES

A recent study applied a relatively simple model to predict the proportion
of workers likely to be community residents in small but rapidly growing Western
communities.[45] The model is based on the following relationships, which are
similar to the variables discussed in the previous section:

1. The proportion of workers who are community residents is inversely

    related to the distance, in road miles (or in time), between the

    community and location of the development.[46] (That is, if a project

    is within a community or close to its boundaries, it is more likely to

    employ local workers than if it is 20 or 30 miles away.)

---

43. See Johnson, Urban Residential Patterns, for a discussion of various
studies on this subject.
44. See Franklin J. James, ed. Models of Employment and Residence
Location, Rutgers University (1974) for a review of these studies.
45. Old West Regional Commission, Construction Worker Profile. Mountain
West Research, Inc. (January 1976 ).
46. Obviously, if "quality" neighborhoods exist close to the location of
new development, housing will be more expensive than in similar neighborhoods
at some distance from centers of employment.

2. The proportion of workers is positively related to the size of the community (or its labor force).

3. The larger the other communities within the development's commuting region (the combined size of noncommunity labor force), the smaller will be the proportion of workers who are community residents.

4. The larger the number of workers from the community already employed in other new developments within the commuting region, the smaller the number to be employed from the community.

Empirical results indicate that about 53 percent of total employment in 14 developments could be explained by the model. This percentage indicates that there are additional factors which affect the proportion of local employees. The model, it should be noted, did not examine the composition of the labor force and compare this composition to the needs of the project. Nor were qualitative differences in community services or population characteristics considered.

E. COST OF ALTERNATIVE METHODS

A major consideration in selecting a method for analysis is the cost involved in obtaining additional information. The use of published data requires little investment. However, much published data, such as that derived from the Census of Population and Housing, becomes obsolete quickly. The use of surveys provides more specific data, particularly if the facilities surveyed are similar to those likely to locate in the community. Essentially, the survey approach is a retrospective analysis. Results can be compared with those which would be predicted on the basis of aggregate data. Since surveys are expensive, it is more efficient for a regional agency rather than a municipality to sponsor such studies. The analytic technique discussed in section D is inexpensive to implement. However, survey data may be necessary to verify the reliability of the estimates, since local conditions may differ from those in communities where the methodology has been determined to be reliable.

F.  INMIGRATION OF WORKERS TO REGION AND THEIR CHOICE OF RESIDENCE

1.  _Proportion of Workers Likely to Inmigrate_.  Similar factors determine
the level of inmigration to a region and the share of new employees that are
residents of the community in which a development locates: the composition
and size of the regional labor force, and the level of regional unemployment.
However, two other factors contribute to the proportion of the labor force
that will inmigrate to a region: organization policy and union policy.  A
business firm can _transfer_ employees or hire workers directly from outside the
region for relocation near the facility.  While some persons may inmigrate to
a growing area in anticipation of finding work, this type of inmigration is
likely to result from the _cumulative_ impact of development rather than from
economic activity generated by a specific development.  Massive projects such
as the Trans-Alaska pipeline are exceptions.

Organizations are likely to transfer top management and highly skilled
high wage personnel, but unskilled, lower wage jobs are usually taken by
local residents, or those residing nearby.

Some national corporations tend to transfer a large number of personnel
to new locations, while others favor the use of local resources.  In addition
to transferring key personnel, organizations also recruit skilled labor from
outside the region.  Again, the availability of skilled labor at competitive
wages within the labor market area probably determines the extent of this
effort. [47]

Union policy, particularly in the construction trades, may require that
a certain number or proportion of the total number of workers required in a
specific category be local union members.  These employees, if available, have
to be given preference.

---

47.  Since corporations generally pay for the cost of relocation, it is
less expensive to hire personnel locally.

2. <u>Characteristics of Inmigrants</u>.  Since employees transferred to or
hired from outside the region are generally more highly trained and educated
than other workers, it is reasonable to assume that construction and other
workers hired from outside the labor market area will have incomes which are
above the level of both locally hired employees and the regional labor force.
Studies of the characteristics of interregional inmigrants confirm that those
moving to a community have a higher socioeconomic status than has the base
population.[48]  However, few studies have examined the characteristics of
workers who migrate in response to demand created by individual developments.
One recent study examined the education and income characteristics of workers
hired for large-scale projects in the energy resources field.  Findings are
presented in Tables I-4 and I-5.  As the data show, nonconstruction worker
inmigrants are twice as likely to have some college education or be college
graduates as the rest of the local labor force.  The median income of construction workers is about $3,700 above the community average, while the in-
come of other inmigrants is about $1,400 higher.  These findings are consistent
with aggregate migration data collected by the Bureau of the Census.[49]

3. <u>Community Choice</u>.  Where do inmigrants choose to reside?  This is an
important issue for planners and policymakers, since estimates of demand for
housing, anticipated tax revenue, and public service demand are based upon
this information.

Aggregate data on inmigration to a region do not distinguish between
those workers likely to reside in the community of new employment and those
electing to live nearby.  Since inmigrants cannot maintain their existing
residences and commute to the facility, they are more likely to select housing

---

48.  U.S., Bureau of the Census, <u>Mobility of the Population of the United
States: March 1970-March 1975</u> (Washington, D.C.: October, 1975).
49.  Ibid.

Table I-4. LEVEL OF EDUCATION OF THE LABOR FORCE
IN SELECTED WESTERN U.S. COMMUNITIES, 1975
(In Percent)

| LEVEL OF EDUCATION | COMMUNITY POPULATION (OTHER THAN INMIGRANTS) | INMIGRANT CONSTRUCTION WORKERS | OTHER INMIGRANTS |
|---|---|---|---|
| Less than High School | 27.1 | 16.6 | 11.8 |
| High School | 43.8 | 45.6 | 32.4 |
| Some College | 13.7 | 21.6 | 28.8 |
| Vocational/Technical School | 2.9 | 7.7 | 3.3 |
| College Graduates (Incl. some Graduate School) | 10.3 | 7.7 | 20.3 |
| Advanced Degree | 2.2 | 0.9 | 3.0 |

Source: Construction Worker Profile.

Table I-5. HOUSEHOLD INCOME OF THE LABOR FORCE IN
SELECTED WESTERN U.S. COMMUNITIES, 1975

| HOUSEHOLD INCOME | COMMUNITY POPULATION (OTHER THAN INMIGRANTS) | INMIGRANT CONSTRUCTION WORKERS | OTHER INMIGRANTS |
|---|---|---|---|
| Less than $6,000 | 14.7 | 0.7 | 4.8 |
| $6,000 to 10,000 | 12.1 | 2.9 | 10.4 |
| $10,000 to 15,000 | 24.1 | 17.7 | 23.4 |
| $15,000 to 25,000 | 39.1 | 57.9 | 50.9 |
| $25,000 and Over | 9.6 | 19.0 | 8.6 |
| No Response | 1.4 | 1.2 | 1.6 |
| Median Income | $13,913 | $17,689 | $15,300 |

Source: Construction Worker Profile.

close to the new development. That is, holding other variables (such as the attractiveness of the community, availability of housing, and cost of housing) constant, people prefer to live close to their jobs. Those who already reside within the region and take new jobs are less likely to move. Their children may be enrolled in school, various social ties would be severed, and the cost of selling a housing unit and moving household goods is high.

Presumably, a large community is more likely to have a broader choice of housing, schools, other public facilities, and private services than a small one. Therefore, holding other factors constant, a large community would attract a bigger share of inmigrants.

A simple mathematical model has been developed to test the hypothesis that the attractiveness of a community as a place of residence of inmigrants is related to (1) the size of the community and (2) the distance separating the community and the new development.[50] The model was tested in a number of Western state communities. The results were mixed, with substantial regional variation among communities. Since the characteristics of each area and large-scale development vary, it may not be feasible to apply a simple model and expect statistically significant results. However, in the absence of other data or insight, this model appears useful as the first step in the estimating procedure. Results derived from this model must be modified to reflect other factors such as the differences in the cost of similar housing, taxes, perceived differences in public services, particularly schools, and related factors. These factors could be added to the model as explanatory variables, or the results could be adjusted to reflect these factors.

---

50. Mountain West Research, Inc., Construction Worker Profile.

## IV.  THE IMPACT OF NEW DEVELOPMENT ON UNEMPLOYMENT

Although it is useful to know the number of new jobs likely to accrue to a community, it is also important to estimate <u>changes</u> in the number of employed, unemployed, and underemployed. New jobs not only expand opportunities for those already working but also provide work for those seeking employment. The motivation for reducing unemployment is economic and social. While the unemployed pay little if any local taxes (other than property), they still need public services. In fact, their demand for social services is likely to increase. Reduced income also hurts local business. Thus, both private and public sector economies are hurt. Several factors, discussed below, determine the impact of expanded work opportunities on the level of unemployment, particularly the type of unemployment in the community and the categories of new jobs created.

A.  <u>EXPANSION OF JOB OPPORTUNITIES AND INMIGRATION</u>

The creation of new jobs in a community or region will not necessarily reduce the number of unemployed. Areas with rapidly expanding employment frequently have <u>higher</u> unemployment levels than communities with a stable level of employment. This results from the inmigration of unemployed persons seeking jobs, especially if the area is known to be one of high wage occupations. For example, Alaska in 1974 had the highest unemployment level in the nation (more than 10 percent) even though jobs increased by 25 percent within a four-year period.[51]  Reports of high paying jobs attracted to Alaska many persons who assumed that jobs were plentiful. Other communities such as San Diego and

---

51. Similarly, California and Florida, both states with net inmigration, had unemployment in 1976 considerably above the national average.

San Francisco also have above average unemployment levels, attributable, in part, to the mild climate and amenities offered in these areas. Many unemployed persons are attracted to such communities, particularly if employment has been growing. At the same time, local residents are less likely to relocate even when job opportunities are reduced.[52] In general, however, cities with population and employment growth, such as Houston, Dallas, or Denver have lower unemployment levels than cities experiencing net outmigration of households and loss of private jobs, such as New York City, St. Louis, Detroit, and Cleveland.

B. TYPES OF UNEMPLOYMENT

To estimate the likely impact of new development on unemployment, it is first necessary to distinguish between various types of unemployment: cyclical, frictional, structural, and hard core.

Cyclical unemployment is typically associated with changes in aggregate spending linked to national recessions. For example, unemployment in the housing and automobile industries during the 1974-1975 recession comes under this category. Thus, the Detroit region had an exceptionally high rate of unemployment in 1975, but the level of unemployment was reduced in 1976 at a faster rate than the national average.

Frictional unemployment is short-term, transitory unemployment. It is part of the normal changes in a dynamic economy which cause people to change jobs and thus be temporarily unemployed. Even at periods of economic expansion, the national unemployment rate is three or more percent. If a large facility leaves a community and some workers are unwilling or unable to relocate, long-term frictional unemployment can result. This category of unemployment is most likely to be reduced through new commercial or industrial development.

---

52. During periods of high national unemployment, some workers from northern manufacturing centers temporarily relocate in areas of milder climate and collect unemployment compensation there.

Structural unemployment is a special kind of frictional unemployment which is reduced by training workers in new skill areas. Help is frequently provided under various federal and state manpower retraining programs. The structually unemployed tend to be out of work for long periods and create serious social as well as economic problems.

Hard-core unemployment is a category comprised of teenagers, the elderly, and minorities who lack basic skills. Such persons often experience difficulty in adapting to the needs of the labor market, even during periods of general economic expansion.

If most unemployment in a community is frictional, the chances of reducing unemployment are considerably high. In a community where unemployment is primarily hard core, new development, unless specifically geared to the needs of this group, is unlikely to have a significant effect on the total number of unemployed or underemployed.

C. FACTORS AFFECTING CHANGE IN UNEMPLOYMENT

The major factor which determines whether unemployment can be reduced is the match between the skills of the unemployed and the needs of new firms. However, even if there is a good match, it should not be assumed that an unemployed person will directly obtain the new position. The unemployed must compete with employed workers who may be interested in changing jobs. Frequently, employed workers are favored over those out of work if the job requires considerable skill. This is based on the premise that the already employed worker is more reliable and has more up-to-date experience.

Union membership can also affect employment status. Unions give preference to their unemployed members, and seniority can determine who a union will recommend for a job.

If a firm relocates or goes out of business, leaving its work force unemployed, the local jurisdiction will attempt to attract a similar facility on the premise that jobs will be filled by the unemployed. However, this is often not feasible, since the industry itself may be declining. The occupation of the unemployed also affects the likelihood of finding suitable industries. In general, unemployment among higher wage jobs (professional, technical, managerial) is lower than for other occupations. For example, during 1971, unemployment for nonfarm laborers averaged 12.8 percent; for craftsmen, 4.9 percent; and for professional and technical workers, only 2.1 percent. Therefore, the chances of reducing unemployment for professional, technical, and skilled labor jobs by attracting new industry are good.

Unemployment is usually higher for teenagers and old workers than others. For these groups, new industrial facilities may not increase their chances of working.

D. OBTAINING DATA ON LOCAL UNEMPLOYMENT

Reliable data about unemployment by areas, occupation, and industry are essential for developing estimates of the effects of new facilities on unemployed residents. While the State Employment Service is a recognized source for this kind of information, maintaining data on unemployment at the county level, such data are generally not grouped by occupation or industry type. Thus other sources must be used.

Computer printouts of state and area unemployment are available, in table format, from the Bureau of the Census _Current Population Estimates_. These tables list the number of unemployed for the largest 30 SMSAs by age, sex, and race. Data by occupation and industry category are not included for individual jurisdictions.

Some states maintain data on unemployment by industry type and occupation for large (one or more county) labor market areas. In California, monthly data on unemployment insurance payments by industry are based on a 20 percent sample of employers. The data are available for large California counties which are also labor market areas (Los Angeles, Orange, Santa Clara, San Diego).

Multi-county data are available for the San Francisco and other labor market

areas. Thus, these areas have information on unemployment by industry.[53]

Data on the number of persons unemployed by occupation, sex, age, and race

are also available for California labor market areas. Such data are particul-

arly useful in estimating development impact. For example, the number of

elementary teachers unemployed in one California county increased from 5 in

1972 to 21 in 1974. This indicates than an expansion in school enrollment

could lower the unemployment rate for elementary teachers in the community.[54]

Similarly, the number of unemployed carpenters increased from 310 in September

1972 to 1,052 in September 1974. Additional construction activity would reduce

this level of unemployment, particularly since unions are likely to favor

local members.

One direct source of data on employment by occupation at the local level

is based on registrants with the State Employment Service's Job Bank Matching

Network in 111 major cities across the country. The Job Bank lists, at a very

detailed (six-digit) occupation description level, both those who register for

jobs with the employment service and job openings listed by employers. The

major limitations of the Job Bank are its coverage of only large cities and

the fact that only a small percentage of unemployed workers and employer

vacancies is listed.

While formal systems which list unemployment by occupation or industry

are limited, local governments can obtain, on an informal basis, data on the

type of unemployment in their community from the local offices of the State

53. California Employment Development Department, Unemployment Insurance Payments by Industry, 96A (February 1975).
54. Usually local teachers involuntarily out of work are given preference over teachers migrating from other areas of the nation.

Employment Service. Local union offices and private employment firms are additional sources of information on unemployment by type.

E.  ESTIMATING THE CHANGE IN THE NUMBER UNEMPLOYED

Direct surveys are the only known way to estimate the number of new jobs filled by the previously underemployed or unemployed at the local level. Because data collected by federal agencies are based on small sample size, results are aggregated at the metropolitan or state level. If new job openings are listed with the State Employment Service (SES) and the agency refers unemployed persons to the new facility, the number of jobs taken can be obtained from the SES. However, since many employers are reluctant to list openings with public agencies, this would provide, at best, only a share of total jobs taken by those unemployed. Surveys of employees, requiring a review of personnel records, are costly and depend on employee cooperation.

A possible indirect measure of the impact of new development at the community level would be to compare the number and occupation of potential new employees likely to live in a jurisdiction with the number of unemployed in the community in each major employment category. For example, if a new facility requires a staff of 200 clerical employees, of whom half are likely to reside in the jurisdiction, and the estimated level of unemployment for these workers in the community is 1,000, a substantial number of clerical persons presently unemployed in the jurisdiction, perhaps as many as 100, would find work. This measure is very crude and should be considered only in the absence of any "hard" data.

F.  EMPIRICAL EVIDENCE

Empirical data on the previous work status of employees in new industrial facilities are limited to a few studies, mostly undertaken in the 1950s and early 1960s. The proportion of previously unemployed workers in the total labor force of three new facilities examined varied from 8 percent of 35 percent.

Studies conducted by the U.S. Department of Commerce's Economic Development

Agency in areas with high local unemployment indicate that 24 percent of workers

in new but subsidized plants were previously unemployed.[55]  Existing studies

focus on facilities in areas of high unemployment, such as Appalachia, or in

facilities subsidized by the federal government.  Therefore, the impact of new

industrial facilities on local unemployment suggested in these studies is

probably not representative of the national pattern.

------

    55.  See William H. Miernyk, "Local Labor Market Effects of New Plant
Locations," Essays in Regional Economics.  Edited by John F. Kain and John R.
Meyer (Cambridge, Mass.: Harvard University Press, 1971) for additional data
on this subject.

# V.  ADDITIONAL ISSUES RELATED TO EMPLOYMENT

A.  REGIONAL SHIFTS IN INDUSTRY LOCATION AND RELATED EMPLOYMENT EFFECTS

Examinations of employment effects associated with new development within local political boundaries are limited, since nationally, many, perhaps a majority of employees do not live and work in the same community.  Therefore, employment issues should be examined at the metropolitan or labor market level. In fact, a major factor in determining whether a county is defined as part of an SMSA is the proportion of its work force that commutes to other jurisdictions. Equally important, a substantial share of new commercial and industrial development, particularly in suburban communities, is comprised of business firms that relocate from another area within the SMSA.  Thus, from the SMSA perspective, there may be no net change in employment but only a redistribution of workers from one site to another.  A study of business firms in New Jersey indicated that over a two-year period, 57 manufacturing firms with 20 or more employees moved from other states; 283, or almost 50 percent, moved within the state; and 262 were newly formed establishments.  Among large new facilities (250 or more employees) none was a new establishment.  Many small and large facilities had relocated within the same county.[56]

A survey of new commercial and industrial facilities in Fairfax County, Virginia, showed that a majority of these facilities relocated from other parts of the SMSA, many from the central city.[57]  As a result, the net regional change

---

56.  N.J., Commuting Patterns.
57.  Hammer, Greene, and Siler Associates, An Industrial Analysis of Fairfax County, prepared for Fairfax County Division of Planning (Washington, D.C.: 1969).

in employment was probably minor. In fact, relocation can, in some cases, result in fewer jobs since new facilities are likely to be more capital inten-[58]sive than the previous facility.

## B. SECOND-ORDER EMPLOYMENT IMPACTS

Increasing primary employment generally has a "multiplier" or second-order job effect since additional workers are required to provide services to those engaged in export-oriented activities.[59]      Secondary employment impact at the local level cannot be reliably estimated. But one technique for developing a loose estimate is for a community to add its aggregate primary (base) and service employment, obtaining a ratio of primary to total jobs. For example, if there are 10,000 primary workers and 18,000 service workers, each additional primary job in the community has resulted in an average of 1.8 service jobs. However, this economic base ratio, at the community level, can be misleading. In an open economy, there is substantial employment "leakage" among the community, the surrounding region, and the balance of the nation. Thus, the ratio may represent typical commuting patterns, with lower wage service workers concentrated in the community, high wage primary workers in a nearby juris- diction. Even in a closed economy, the historical pattern may not be mean- ingful in projecting future employment. Thus, service jobs have been growing more rapidly than industrial employment. Factors influencing the ratio between primary and "second-order" employment include the income level of primary workers. High wage primary employment, other factors held constant, will result in a higher ratio of nonprimary workers than primary employment with low average wages.

---

58. The number of employees per dollar of sales in newer suburban fac- ilities is lower than in central cities.

59. It may be that, in the long run, a high level of private and public services could also attract more export-oriented firms.

One example of the economic base approach to estimate secondary employment is presented in a study of the Washington, D.C., SMSA.[60] Based on a cross-sectional analysis of regional employment, the study assumes that for every federal government job (defined as primary employment in the region) there are 2.3 nonprimary jobs, including 0.3 of a job at the local and state government level and 0.2 job in construction. However, as the study notes, the ratio is based on somewhat arbitrary assumptions.

Some local governments estimate the ratio of industrial to other jobs and the number of industrial jobs based on land use. For example, the city of San Jose estimates that each industrial job creates approximately 2.6 other jobs in commerce, education, government, and service categories.[61] The city also estimates that there are 20 industrial jobs per acre of industrially developed land. Since 1.2 workers per household are assumed, the city concludes that each industrially developed acre "supports" 60 households.[62]

Data collected by the U.S. Chamber of Commerce based on a sample of ten rural counties show the following relationship between new manufacturing jobs and other employment: every 100 manufacturing jobs will generate 21 jobs in wholesale and retail trade, 17 professional or related service jobs, 11 jobs in transportation and other utilities, and 19 other jobs.[63] On this basis, every primary manufacturing job is accompanied by 0.68 secondary manufacturing job. The methodology and classification in this report differ from other studies, making it impossible to compare the results.

---

60. Hammer, Greene, and Siler, The Economy of Metropolitan Washington (Washington, D.C.: Washington Metropolitan Council of Governments, 1969).

61. City of San Jose, Urban Growth and Development Policies, revised draft (1974).

62. This approach has several limitations, among them the assumption that the present ratio of industrial to nonindustrial workers reflects future development.

63. What New Jobs Mean to a Community (Washington, D.C.: Chamber of Commerce of the United States, 1973).

In general, multipliers used by local governments tend to exaggerate the impact of new industrial and commercial development on secondary employment. One empirical analysis shows that a garment factory in Arkansas had an estimated local multiplier effect (local and nonlocal) of only 1.6.[64]

As noted previously, some new development, especially shopping centers, shift employment within a jurisdiction or region. As residential development moves outward from the center of a city, commercial development follows. A retail store in an older neighborhood moves, with its employees, to a new shopping mall. This relocation, which transfers employees to a newer facility, has little impact on aggregate community or regional employment. In fact, unless the new facility anticipates greater sales, fewer employees may be required at the new facility.

Input-output tables provide one way of estimating secondary employment by calculating the employment linkage between one industry and others. An input-output model of a region, for example, can provide a distribution of occupations by industry and an estimate of secondary employment which would result from a new industry. This technique is limited however. Only a few metropolitan areas have input-output tables based on regional linkages. The smaller the geographic area, the less reliable are input-output table coefficients, particularly coefficients based on national data.

The approach suggested in this report is for local governments to estimate only two categories of secondary employment generated by new development directly: municipal workers and construction employment, but to exclude other secondary employment since this could result in "double counting." For example, the impact of a new residential development on additional demand for

---

64. Max F. Jordan, <u>Industrialization in the Ozarks-A Case Study</u>, Agricultural Economic Report, no. 123, Washington, D.C.: U.S. Department of Agriculture, November 1967).

services could be estimated.  The demand could then be converted into additional service employment.  However, if one also examines employment effects of a shopping center or an office building in the community, the same services, employment may be counted twice.  Other reasons for excluding multiple impacts include the imprecise nature of secondary employment effects from the local level and the difficulty in distinguishing between primary and secondary jobs.

C.  ESTIMATING THE EMPLOYMENT IMPACT OF PUBLIC INVESTMENT

The expansion of public sector capital investment increases the importance of estimating its employment impact, particularly the importance to local and state officials.  In some instances, such data are necessary to obtain federal "impact aid."  For example, Kitsap County and nearby counties near Seattle, Washington, are eligible for certain federal funds if it is found that a large military facility and new jobs associated with the facility have an adverse fiscal impact on the area.  Estimating the level of primary and secondary employment as well as the previous residence of workers generated by the new project is crucial to the process of estimating the economic impact of public investment.

San Francisco is currently examining the economic impact of the BART mass transit system by estimating the level and income of secondary employment presumably created from this multibillion dollar investment.  In studies involving local or regional public investment, it is necessary to consider the reduction in taxpayers' disposable income to pay for new facilities and the employment effects of lower disposable income.[65]

---

65.  Joel Bergsman, Thomas Muller, Bob McGillivray, Harvey Garn, "Development of Methodology for the Assessment of BART's Impact Upon Economics and Finances" (Washington, D.C.: The Urban Institute, October 17, 1974).

D. <u>ESTIMATING THE FUTURE PATTERN OF EMPLOYMENT AT THE COMMUNITY</u> LEVEL

The previous sections of this report concentrated on estimating new employment after a business firm has selected a specific site for constructing a facility. However, planners are frequently interested in estimating the future level of employment. Thus, an alternative approach is to estimate the likely <u>demand</u> for commercial and industrial land at the community level, and derive aggregate employment estimates from the land use information. For example, most comprehensive plans designate certain areas for industrial and commercial land uses. It is thus important to know the types of facilities and subsequent levels of employment a community can anticipate at these designated sites.

In discussing the location of industrial facilities, two decisions made by most business firms must be discussed. The first involves whether to locate in a particular metropolitan area or nonmetropolitan region; the second involves selecting a specific site in a community within the general area.[66]

Numerous studies have examined factors which determine the locational choice of business firms.[67] In addition, the American Truck Association, <u>Fortune</u> magazine, and others have surveyed firms to determine key factors which influenced their site selection decision. The most frequently noted factors among organizations surveyed are availability of workers, proximity to consumers, proximity to transportation (particularly highways and rail service), and the availability of suitable land. In addition, highly personal motivations (the head of a corporation may select a community because it is close to a preferred place of residence) can play a role in the site selection process.

---

66. See, for example, T. E. McMillan "Why Manufacturers Choose Plant Locations vs. Determinants of Plant Location," <u>Land Economics</u> (March 1965).
67. In the case of federal facilities, all taxpayers nationally share in the cost. Therefore, the effect on local taxpayers is minimal.

General data from surveys are typically used to estimate the likelihood of particular industry groupings locating in a community.[68] This procedure uses the site selection factors cited above to compare the relative locational advantage of the community vis-a-vis competing communities in the region. Each factor is assigned both a maximum weight (reflecting its relative importance) and a measure of local conditions, ranging from 0 (seriously deficient) to 1.00 (greatly superior). For example, the item "cost and availability of central gas compared to its neighbors" is assigned a maximum weight of 0.06 and a local condition measure of 0.8 (superior). Thus, its score is 0.06 x 0.8, or 0.048.[69] Similarly, wage rates have a maximum weight of 0.05, and community attitudes, 0.04. The maximum aggregate weight of _all_ factors equals 1.0. If by using this methodology, a community produced an aggregate total score of 0.60, it could assume that it is in a better competitive position to attract a particular category of industry than a neighboring community with an aggregate total score of 0.40.

A major limitation of factor weighting is that there is frequently little difference between factor weights within a region. Utility rates and wages tend to be uniform, and communities operate in the same labor and consumer market. Even if a community receives a high score, there is little assurance that it will attract a particular type of industry.

No calibrated model exists to predict future industrial location at the community level with reliability. Some communities, to increase the likelihood of obtaining new industry, provide substantial incentives, such as tax abatement, leasing industrial space at low rates, and employment training programs.

---

68. Decision Sciences Corporation, _Advanced New Community Simulation System_ (Jenkintown, Pa.: October 1973).

69. A local condition score of 0.2 (deficient) would result in a score for natural gas of 0.012.

However, there is a tendency for adjoining communities to "match" these incentives. If such competition takes place, jurisdictions will probably increase taxes to pay for these incentives with little, if any, visible benefit to the community.

The most common method for estimating the future location of retail stores is a modified form of the gravity model, which assumes that dollar outlays in a retail zone decrease in proportion to the increased distance (travel time) from the residence of a household. Since people are most likely to shop near their residence, retail outlets, particularly for convenience goods, follow new residential development. If the purchasing power of new households is known, the sales volume for goods and services can be predicted and converted to employment estimates. This approach is useful for convenience goods, such as food markets, which locate in new residential development. The specific location of regional shopping centers and specialty goods stores is more difficult to predict, although accessibility is known to be a major factor in their location. Planners in each community may zone large parcels of land for "industrial" or "commercial" use, but there is little assurance that business firms will locate in these areas. Since each community hopes to attract new industry, this accounts, in part, for the oversupply of commercially and industrially zoned land found in many jurisdictions.

Commercial growth at the regional level, in terms of both shopping facilities and office space, can be estimated by using data on population growth and the increase in real disposable personal income per household. However, regional projections are of limited use at the local level unless it is assumed that a community will receive a certain percentage of total growth based on its historical share.

It is difficult to estimate the future level of nonmarket-oriented
industries, even at the regional level, although the U.S. Department of
Commerce recently projected the level of future (1980 and 1990) export-
oriented employment for all SMSAs. This projection was based on the assumption
that the share of each industrial sector in the metropolitan area will follow
the historical pattern.[70] Industrial facilities such as food processing, with
a competitive advantage if located near population centers, are likely to locate
or expand existing facilities in a region as its population and real income
increase. Thus, growing areas are likely to attract such facilities, independent of local initiatives. Other industries which depend on a supply of raw
materials, cheap energy, or a low-wage labor force can rarely be attracted
to a region lacking these characteristics regardless of tax or other incentives.

The major component of personal income is derived from wages and salaries.
Therefore, an increase in the number of jobs held by present community residents,
or an increase in average wages for those already in the labor force, causes a
substantial increase in aggregate and per capita personal income. The addition
of households from other areas attracted by new employment opportunities can
increase or reduce per capita income, depending on whether the income of new
residents is above or below the national community average. Typically, however,
areas with net inmigration experience a more rapid rise in per capita income
than stable communities or those with population decline, since inmigrants
have a higher income than the community average.[71]

70. See U.S., Department of Commerce Bureau of Economic Analysis, Area
Economic Projections for 1990 (Washington, D.C.: 1974). Population, personal
income and other employment data are derived from the assumed level of export-
oriented jobs. The projections are adjusted, in some cases, based on judgment
regarding local conditions.
71. For a discussion of inmigration, see Muller, Growing and Declining
Urban Areas.

An increase in local employment, even if most workers commute to the jurisdiction, has a positive effect on local retail store sales and will contribute to the earnings of proprietors. Similarly, local banks and other financial institutions benefit from growth. In some instances, however, more competition results because new private businesses are attracted to the community. Further, those living on a fixed income may be adversely affected since the cost of living is likely to rise as a result of rapid economic expansion.

# VI.  FINDINGS AND RECOMMENDATIONS

## A.  ESTIMATING THE NUMBER OF JOBS CREATED BY NEW DEVELOPMENT

In the absence of local surveys it is possible, by using the techniques discussed or referred to in this report, to estimate four categories of employment associated with new development: short-term private and public jobs, and long-term private and public jobs.  Local governments should limit their analysis to direct employment, unless municipal job changes attributable to growth are being estimated.

## B.  ESTIMATING THE SHARE OF JOBS TAKEN BY LOCAL RESIDENTS

In contrast to the straightfoward approaches used to estimate total employment, there are no generally acceptable methods for estimating the residence of those employed in new commercial or industrial facilities. Models which include two or three variables may be useful as an initial approach if they include adjustments which reflect the judgmental factor. Existing studies indicate that higher income workers may commute to newly built facilities from substantial distances, or many inmigrate to the area from other regions in response to new employment opportunities.  Thus, the number of new jobs taken by local residents, particularly if the community is within a metropolitan area, may represent a small share of the total number of job openings created.  The characteristics of the local work force, the level of unemployment, and the size of the community are among those factors influencing the number of local workers taking new jobs.

## C.  UNEMPLOYMENT AND UNDEREMPLOYMENT

The short-term impact of new employment opportunities on existing local unemployment depends primarily on the type of unemployment in the community and the characteristics of the labor force required by new firms.  In some instances, the number of unemployed may actually increase if high wage jobs are expanding in a community. More typically, however, growth in employment opportunities will reduce the overall level of unemployment.

## D. EMPLOYMENT FROM THE REGIONAL PERSPECTIVE

The impact of land development on employment, housing, income and other areas can be assessed with greater reliability at the regional rather than local level, since where people work, live, and spend their earnings is generally not limited by political boundaries. Frequently, new industrial or commercial facilities result in minimal net regional employment since firms locating in new facilities may have abandoned structures in other parts of the region. In such cases, the labor force simply changes its commuting patterns and does not expand.

## E. SECONDARY EMPLOYMENT EFFECTS

Communities and local business organizations frequently cite substantial gains in secondary employment among the major benefits which derive from new commercial or industrial facilities. This increase is based on the "multiplier" effect which results from service and other jobs created by the addition of "primary" employment. At the local level, this concept is difficult to translate into net employment gains. Therefore, with the exception of the local public sector, second-order employment estimates should be considered only at the regional level.

## F. FUTURE LEVEL AND TYPE OF EMPLOYMENT

Many communities project the aggregate level of future employment as part of their long-range planning process. However, it is extremely difficult to predict, with any accuracy, future growth levels in specific industries which do not depend on local natural resources or the local market. Aggregate future commercial development and employment, particularly net additional growth (new facilities less those abandoned or demolished), depends primarily on the overall level of population growth and changes in disposable personal income. Estimates, in turn, depend considerably on the ability to project future level of industrial and other export-oriented developments.

G. THE QUALITY OF EMPLOYMENT DATA AT THE LOCAL LEVEL

Information on local employment and unemployment conditions is typically limited. Data gathered by federal agencies are focused at the metropolitan level, except for the decennial census, which quickly becomes obsolete, and special surveys. Information on the supply and demand for jobs, other than data derived from local employment advertising and data provided by public or private employment agencies, is also limited.

In Florida, sponsors of large-scale developments are required to provide information on the number of jobs, wages, and the likely residence of the anticipated work force. In the absence of baseline data, local or regional planning staffs cannot verify the reliability of the figures provided. This report suggests ways to estimate the level of employment if the characteristics of new developments are known. The use of these methods in Florida and elsewhere would be strengthened by surveys, particularly concerning the previous residence of workers by region and type.

PART II—THE IMPACT OF NEW DEVELOPMENT ON HOUSING

# I. INTRODUCTION AND BACKGROUND

A. <u>RELATIONSHIP BETWEEN HOUSING AND COMPREHENSIVE IMPACT EVALUATION</u>

The demand for housing is directly linked to nonresidential development that creates new <u>employment</u> opportunities and increases personal income. The construction of new housing also affects the tax base and the demand for public services, and thus has a major fiscal impact on the community. Since housing requires considerably more land than commercial or industrial development, increased housing demand has a substantial effect on <u>land values</u>.

The natural environment is affected by new housing insofar as housing increases population, and subsequently the use of transportation facilities, the level of sewerage, and the demand for water. If new housing changes the demographic or socioeconomic population distribution, it can have <u>social</u> effects on the community.

B. <u>OBJECTIVES OF HOUSING IMPACT STUDIES</u>

From the community standpoint, construction of new housing can have a number of positive effects. It provides short-term construction employment, increases the choice of housing for community residents, and may release part of the older housing stock to those who cannot afford new housing. However, residential development can also have negative effects. Among these are adverse fiscal impacts if revenue generated by new housing falls short of service costs imposed by new residents; increased pollution, primarily as a result of an increase in population; and social tension if new residents differ substantially in income or living style from the existing community average.[1] Occupants of new housing, regardless of the fiscal balance, can cause, at least in the short run, additional traffic congestion and overcrowded public facilities such as recreation centers and schools. Finally, land-intensive housing projects reduce future development options by curtailing the available supply of unimproved land.

In the absence of adverse effects, there is little need to estimate the impact of new residential development on the housing needs of a community. If the private market will invest in new housing, even if community residents do not live in such units, public land use decisions should not be affected. While a jurisdiction may prefer a wider choice of housing for its residents, it could not reasonably object to housing aimed at a nonlocal market. However, new residential development is likely to have some adverse impact on the community. Thus, the community should analyze proposed residential development to determine the degree to which the new housing will

1.  expand housing choices for residents,

2.  meet directly the need for housing among inadequately housed residents,

3.  release part of the old housing stock to those in need of housing,

4.  overburden public facilities.[2]

---

1.  None of these adverse effects necessarily takes place. A residential development can have a positive fiscal effect, cause no overcrowding, and have only a marginal impact on pollution. Differences in socioeconomic characteristics do not necessarily create social problems.

2.  This is the subject of other Urban Institute reports in this series.

Other potentially positive effects of housing are examined as part of this impact analysis series. These included positive fiscal benefits, discussed in a previous publication, and expanded short-term employment opportunities discussed in Part I of this report.

C. THE LOCAL AND REGIONAL PERSPECTIVE

Since many families will reside in one community and work in another, the housing market area corresponds spatially to the labor market area.[3] As such, the housing market area almost always extends beyond the political boundaries of a community. Therefore, examinations of housing supply and demand from a local perspective are limited. The construction of a large industrial facility can have a substantial effect on housing demand in adjacent communities. At the same time, the construction of a large residential development in a nearby jurisdiction can reduce the demand for housing in a community. Nonetheless, as in other reports in this series, attention is focused on the community level, since most land use decisions are made locally. Regional considerations are typically less important than local interests in land use policies and decisions, since local officials respond primarily to the needs and preferences of their constituents.

_____

3. In some central cities, such as Washington, D.C., commuters comprise more than half of the total city work force.

## II.  IMPACT OF DEVELOPMENT
## ON HOUSING SUPPLY AND DEMAND

New residential housing, both owner-occupied and rental units, will increase the supply of housing.  However, the impact of new units on local
residents will depend on the type and other characteristics of the new
housing.  Therefore, the first step in an analysis is to compare the
characteristics of new housing to the existing housing stock.  New units
can affect residents directly by providing additional housing options, or
indirectly by releasing older units.

The demand for housing is increased by commercial and industrial
development, which expands employment opportunities and increases personal
income.  This in turn stimulates the effective demand for housing.  However,
as noted later, some unsatisfied, or noneffective, demand is likely to
persist despite a rise in economic activity.

A.  OWNER-OCCUPIED AND RENTAL UNITS

In the discussion of housing impact, a basic distinction is made
between units that are owner-occupied and those that are rented.  Two
major characteristics make this division significant:

    1.  Variances in average income, household size, and age distribution;

    2.  Differences in the proportion of income allocated to housing.

The market for owner-occupied housing is typically concentrated in
detached, single-family units.  While townhouses and highrise condominiums
have recently competed for a share of the market, the dominant share of
owner-occupied housing (in fact of all housing) in 1975 consisted of
detached units.  Some detached units are renter occupied, although the

initial resident is likely to have been the owner.[4]

Rental units are dominated by apartments, generally defined as buildings with four or more housing units. Typically, these units are smaller and less costly to maintain than owner-occupied, detached housing. The average income of residents of rental units is lower than the average income of residents of detached housing. Rental units are more likely to attract temporary residents, young households without children, singles, and the aged. Residents of public housing, other than the elderly, have larger households due to more children per household than occupants of nonsubsidized rental units.

Mobile housing comprises a large segment of owner-occupied units among lower income households. These units also appeal to some middle-income families, and are particularly attractive to temporary residents.

B. HOUSING SUPPLY CHANGES

1. Comparing New Units to the Existing Housing Stock. Developers applying for rezoning or building permits provide data on the number of units to be constructed by type, the number of bedrooms or square feet per unit, and plans to sell or rent the units. While information on the selling price or monthly rentals may not be formally requested, most builders will informally provide it if it is not released publicly. Even if such information is unavailable, the price or rental range can be estimated by using information based on similar, already occupied housing.

---

4. For data on the proportion of detached housing units rented as a percentage of all such units, see U.S., Bureau of the Census, 1970 Census of Population and Housing.

Information on the total number of dwelling units by type (single family, townhouse, apartment) is frequently maintained by the local planning department or by the department responsible for property tax assessment. Using assessor's records, the selling price of units by type can be estimated by converting assessed value to market value on the basis of a ratio which is based on comparing the selling price of housing to its assessed value.[5] A more direct source of market value, based on recent sales, can be obtained from local realtors. Data on rents are more difficult to obtain and usually require surveys of apartment managers.

A comparison of the type, price range, and monthly rental of new housing units with the existing housing stock provides an initial assessment of whether proposed units will differ substantially from the present housing stock and how the new residential development will alter the composition of the stock.

2. Filtering of the Housing Stock. New residential units, in addition to expanding the housing stock, can indirectly affect the housing needs of a community. The process of filtering, or the passing of a housing unit from use by the household for which it was originally built to one with different income and other socioeconomic characteristics, is one of the most significant secondary effects. Generally the process works downward. As a result of physical deterioration, economic factors, and social forces, a housing unit can decline in value relative to other housing of its type. These factors enable households with lower incomes to purchase or rent housing that its original occupants could not buy. "Filtering up" generally

5. For example if the average unit price of 10 single family dwellings sold in a community is $60,000 and their assessed value $20,000, the assessed to market value ratio is 0.33.

takes place in areas where location, historical significance, quality of housing, or other factors create an increased demand for older housing. Examples of this process are the Georgetown and Capitol Hill sections of Washington, D.C., which were once low-income areas.

The importance of filtering can be demonstrated by examining the quantity and cost of new housing. The average age of a private housing unit in the nation is 27 years. Since the total number of available units in existence at the end of 1973 was 76 million, the 2 million units built during this boom construction year added only 2.6 percent to the total housing stock.[6] Thus, the probability of a household being able to buy or rent a new unit, particularly a household with an income close to or below the median, is low since the average purchase and rental prices of new housing are higher than the average prices of existing units.

In 1973, a typical new detached housing unit sold for $38,500, while an existing unit sold for $31,800, or 21 percent less.[7] Since the mean household income in the U.S. in 1973 was $12,100, a typical household could hardly afford to purchase a new detached unit. In fact, less than 30 percent of all households in 1973 had an income sufficiently high to qualify for a mortgage with a 20 percent down payment.

While the concept of "filtering down" is sound, those studying the housing market disagree about the extent to which the process actually takes

---

6. About 0.5 million units were taken out of the market in 1973. Thus, the net addition during the year was only 1.5 million units.

7. The average purchase price of FHA-insured new homes in 1974 was estimated to be $27,000, existing homes $22,000. The source of property value data is the U.S. Department of Housing and Urban Development and the U.S. Bureau of the Census.

place. Since housing demand is closely linked to general economic conditions in an area and the quality of housing stock differs substantially among areas, it is difficult to develop a method for measuring the potential effects of new expensive housing units on the availability of older, inexpensive apartments. Given substantial inmigration, the supply, regardless of the level of construction activity, may not exceed demand. In this case, filtering down would not occur. In older areas with stable populations or areas experiencing outmigration of middle income households, such as in many central cities, the filtering down process probably occurs.[8]

Filtering down is caused, in part, by physical deterioration. The rate of deterioration, in turn, depends on two factors: durability of the building material and the degree of maintenance. For example, structures built of stone or brick are likely to deteriorate more slowly than those built primarily of wood. The quality of construction, regardless of building materials used, affects the speed of deterioration. The level of maintenance itself is affected by neighborhood characteristics. Thus, the addition of polluting industrial facilities can reduce the value of adjoining residential property and accelerate the filtering process. In contrast, the addition of parks and schools will probably enhance the value of existing units. Changes in economic conditions have made large Victorian units costly to maintain, frequently resulting in inadequate up-keep. Tenement type housing (defined as buildings with three or more stories with no elevators, poor lighting and bad ventilation), even if well constructed, is considered undesirable as the standard of living increases.

---

8. See John B. Lansing et al., New Homes and Poor People (Ann Arbor: University of Michigan, Survey Research Center, 1969) for an empirical study of filtering.

Thus, these structures are likely to be poorly maintained, accelerating the rate of deterioration.

If "filtering down" takes place, the construction of new units should cause at least some households in a community to relocate from older units to new ones. At the end of this lengthy process, a housing unit in an older, less desirable area of the jurisdiction will be vacated and may become available to a household with insufficient income to purchase or rent a new and more expensive unit.

While the concept of filtering is generally accepted, it is rarely included in housing models. An exception is a simulation of the San Francisco region housing market, which incorporates this concept.[9]

C. CHANGES IN HOUSING DEMAND

1. Effective and Noneffective Demand. Demand for housing can be divided into two categories: effective (private market) demand and noneffective (nonmarket) demand. Effective demand represents the level of demand for adequate housing which can be met without public subsidies, taking into account income, age, and household size. Noneffective demand requires that households obtain subsidies or housing allowances to occupy adequate housing.

The line between what households can or cannot afford to pay for housing is somewhat arbitrary. However, it is obvious that a 70-year-old couple with a total income of $200 per month and no savings cannot afford adequate private market housing in a metropolitan area. This is clearly an example of noneffective demand. Without public subsidies, this couple is

9. Jobs, People and Land: Bay Area Simulation Study, Special Report No. 6 (Berkeley, University of California, 1968).

therefore likely to be inadequately housed. Similarly, the demand for housing for a family with six children and an income of $500 per month is noneffective.

While this report concentrates on estimating housing needs for households with incomes sufficient for private market housing, low-income households in need of housing should not be ignored. The method used by communities such as Los Angeles to estimate noneffective demand assumes that a household cannot reasonably allocate more than 25 percent of its gross (pre-tax) income for housing. Using this criterion, Los Angeles determined that 44 percent of its households are paying "excessive rent" for housing.[10] Further, while 80 percent of low-income households pay too much for rent, so do 14 percent of high-income households. Obviously, high-income households _prefer_ to pay more for housing than for other discretionary purchases. This illustrates how a percentage of income criterion can be misleading in attempting to estimate noneffective housing demand.

2. <u>Impact of Commercial and Industrial Development</u>. The extent to which new commercial and industrial development increases the <u>demand</u> for housing in the short run depends on the number of households that inmigrate to the community from other areas because of new facilities. In the absence of inmigration (i.e., workers either commute from other jurisdictions or are already community residents), demand for housing may not increase immediately. Over time, however, the demand for housing linked to nonresidential development would increase as a result of the following three conditions:

<u>Rise in personal income</u>. In the absence of immediate inmigration, resident employees are typically entering (or reentering) the labor market,

---

10. Los Angeles Community Analysis Bureau. <u>The Los Angeles Housing Model - Technical Report</u> (July 1974) Statistics in the report are based on <u>1970 Census of Housing</u>.

currently unemployed, or in the process of changing jobs. In all three cases, disposable income is likely to rise. This, in turn, will increase the demand for housing.[11]

Second-order impact. If residents change jobs, their vacated positions will probably be taken by others. Such interrelated job changes, in turn, will probably cause additional inmigration, unless employment in other economic sectors within the community, has been reduced and workers from these facilities transferred or unemployment is being reduced.

Additional employment. New facilities employing workers with rising income will generate a need for goods and services. The expanded demand may also trigger some inmigration.[12]

Changes in demand for housing over time which are attributable to secondary employment are difficult to determine. Therefore, only primary changes in housing demand should be estimated, noting that these changes represent short-term effects of new development.

Increases in income attributable to new employment and the subsequent overall expansion of economic activity will also accelerate the abandonment or upgrading of marginal, substandard housing, particularly if there is little inmigration and if rising housing demand is met through an increase in residential construction. Additional employment resulting from new commercial and industrial development will increase aggregate wages and

---

11. See Frank deLeeuw, "The Demand for Housing: A Review of Cross-Section Evidence," Review of Economic and Statistics (February 1971) for studies of housing demand elasticity.

12. For discussion of the likelihood that newly created jobs will be taken by local residents, see Part I of this report.

salaries directly.[13] As was shown earlier in this chapter, it is difficult to

estimate both the level of inmigration to a community and housing demand attrib-

utable to new households. Sudden increases in employment are believed to have

an upward effect on the price of the existing housing stock as additional

households and higher income levels serve to stimulate higher prices. Some

communities are unwilling, for fiscal, social, and other reasons, to pro-

vide the new housing necessary to meet expanding demands. In such cases,

higher prices may be permanent. Even if new construction balances the

housing supply and demand, housing will be more costly, on the average, as

added income works through the local economy, increasing wages of

construction workers, expanding profit margins for contractors and builders,

and raising the price of undeveloped land. However, as noted earlier,

restricting housing in the face of higher demand will further accelerate

housing costs. A restrictive policy benefits those owning improved

property in the community, since demand for new housing will exceed its supply,

to the detriment of those seeking to purchase or rent housing and to owners

of unimproved land, since its value may drop if growth is restricted.

---

13. Development sponsored by the government, such as space centers, missile sites, and other installations, have essentially the same economic impact as private development, although fiscal effects may differ since government property is tax exempt.

# III.  METHODS TO ESTIMATE COMMUNITY DEMAND

This section discusses the methods that can be used to estimate characteristics of housing occupants, such as income and demographic profiles.  Reports published by the U.S. Bureau of the Census and related sources are used.  Changes in the relationship between household characteristics and housing demand between 1970 and 1974 are noted, and a method for estimating demand is described.

A.  GENERAL DATA SOURCES

1.  Income.  Typically, the share of income customarily allocated by households in a particular income group for housing is used as the basis for estimating the value of housing required in a community or region.  However, the use of income as the only determinant of housing demand is limited by the following factors:

1.  In an inflationary period, a higher than average share of income may be allocated for owner-occupied housing, the purchase of which is treated as a form of savings with certain tax advantages.[14]

2.  Income is generally defined as current income, although housing consumption is also linked to average (lifetime) income.

3.  The ages of household members are linked to the ability to pay for housing.  Thus, students or retirees can afford to allocate a higher proportion of their income to housing than a household with school-age children.

---

14.  See George Peterson, Federal Tax Policy and Urban Development (Washington, D.C.: The Urban Institute, 1976 (draft), for a discussion of tax implications associated with housing demand.

Households with identical socioeconomic and demographic characteristics place different values on housing (have different tastes) vis-a-vis other discretionary outlays such as food, services, or travel.

Although these limitations must be recognized, income remains a pivotal determinant in housing demand. Therefore, changes in local income are used to estimate housing demand. The only available source of income data for all communities in the nation since the 1970 census, which includes data on 1969 income, is the Population Estimates and Projections Series published by the U.S. Bureau of the Census.[15] Data in this series are limited to two items: total income and mean per capita income. Personal aggregate and per capita income are also available on an annual basis for counties from the Survey of Current Business.[16] Neither of these sources, unfortunately, provides information on the income distribution of community residents, which is available only from the census for multistate regions based on annual surveys. Since local data are unavailable unless surveys have been taken, it can be assumed, in the absence of major economic changes in the community since 1970, that the rise in income in the region should be proportional in each income group. If average income in a community has been increasing faster than for the region as a whole, then the proportion of households in higher income categories has, in most instances, also increased at a rate exceeding the national average. Step-by-step procedures for updating the income distribution in a community based on community wage data are contained in a HUD

15. U.S., Bureau of the Census, Population Estimates and Projections, series P-25.

16. U.S.,Bureau of Economic Analysis, Survey of Current Business. The definition of income differs from the one used by the U.S. Bureau of the Census. For definition of personal income, see Survey of Current Business (May 1974), l. This issue also lists personal income by source for all counties and SMSAs in the nation during 1972.

publication.[17]  The most current income data from the U.S. Bureau of the Census annual surveys should be substituted in the formulas for wage data if the FHA approach is used to estimate the income distribution at the community or SMSA level.

Except for data by income category in the 1970 Census of Population, only per capita income data are available at the local level for more recent years.  Since household size has changed, household income should not be estimated by multiplying more current per capita values by the average 1970 household size.  The most recent estimates of household size, discussed on page 97, should be used for these estimates.  If the total number of occupied residential units is know (total units less vacancies) this value should be divided by total money income to obtain average household income at the local level.

A major problem in using most 1970 census data stems from the failure to distinguish between income characteristics of new housing and the total housing stock.  This can lead to a misconception that the demographic and economic characteristics of households moving into new housing do not differ significantly from the community average.  In developing estimates of the impact of new housing on community housing needs, it is useful to examine differences between new and existing units and recent changes in housing consumption.

2.  Demographic Characteristics.  Several indirect techniques can be used to estimate the current age distribution of community residents.  In the absence of substantial inmigration or outmigration,  1970 Census of

17.  FHA Techniques of Housing Market Analysis, FHA Circular 1380.2 (Washington, D.C.:  Department of Housing and Urban Development, January 1970).

Population data can be updated by using the cohort-survival technique to add birth and death information from the county level. Changes in the proportion of school-age children of the total population can be obtained from current public and private school enrollments. These data can then be compared to total population change since 1970.[18] Changes in the average household size can also be estimated by dividing the total number of occupied dwelling units by the total population. Information on the number of AFDC recipients, the number of social security recipients, and similar social data can be obtained from HEW. Age distribution by state for 1974 is available from the U.S. Census Current Population Estimates series.

B. DATA FROM THE SURVEY OF HOUSING

1. Characteristics of New Housing Occupants. As shown in Tables II-I and II-2, demographic and economic characteristics of new housing occupants are based on national averages derived from the Annual Housing Survey which provides detailed data. However, the same data categories are available by region and grouped by central cities, suburbs, and nonmetropolitan areas within each region in the referenced data source. While characteristics of a community may differ from regional patterns, major deviations are unlikely. Thus, the use of this data source can provide useful information on changes since the last decennial Census.

Single-person households, as shown in the Annual Housing Survey, are most likely to rent rather than purchase housing, while households 65 years of age or older, with less mobility, are unlikely either to rent or purchase

18. Some states, such as Virginia, conduct surveys of persons 18 years or younger in each school district regardless of school attendance.

TABLE II-1. DEMOGRAPHIC CHARACTERISTICS OF HOUSEHOLDS IN THE UNITED STATES, 1973

| HOUSEHOLD CHARACTERISTICS | OWNER-OCCUPIED | | RENTAL-OCCUPIED | |
|---|---|---|---|---|
| | All Housing | New Housing | All Housing | New Housing |
| 2 or More Persons (%) | 86 | 93 | 69 | 70 |
| Male Headed, 2 or More Persons (%) | 91 | 95 | 70 | 86 |
| 65 or Over, 1 or More Persons (%) | 24 | 7 | 16 | 9 |
| Children Under 18 (%) | 46 | 62 | 37 | 33 |
| Children Only Under 6 (%) | 8 | 21 | 14 | 15 |
| Both Child Age Categories (%) | 10 | 16 | 8 | 6 |
| Median Number of Occupants | 2.8 | 3.2 | 2.1 | 2.0 |

SOURCE: U.S., Bureau of the Census, Annual Housing Survey: 1973, part A, (July 1975).

TABLE  II-2. ECONOMIC CHARACTERISTICS OF U.S. HOUSEHOLDS, 1973

| ECONOMIC CHARACTERISTICS | OWNER-OCCUPIED | | RENTAL-OCCUPIED | |
|---|---|---|---|---|
| | All Housing | New Housing | All Housing | New Housing |
| Median Income (1973) | $12,800 | $13,800 | $7,700 | $10,200 |
| Income $15,000 or More (1972) (%) | 40 | 34 | 17 | 22 |
| Median House Value/ Gross Rent | $27,200 | $36,300 | $148 | $186 |
| Ratio of Median House Value to Median Income a/ | 2.12 | 2.63 | 23% | 22% |
| House Value to Income Ratio, 2.5 or More | 37 | 35 b/ | -- | -- |
| Rent 25% or More of Income (% Rental Units) | --- | --- | 42 | 42 |

SOURCE:   U.S.,Bureau of the Census, Annual Housing Survey:  1973, part A (July 1975).

a/  For rental units, the annual rent as a percentage of income is calculated.

b/  House Value to Income Ratio, 3.0 or more (2.5 or more not computed for new housing).

new units. Holding income <u>constant</u>, a large family is more likely to own than rent. For example, households with incomes of $25,000 or more who own their housing have 3.8 persons; those who rent, 2.4 persons.

The likelihood that families moving into new owner-occupied housing will have children from the ages of 6 to 18 is substantially higher than the probability of children residing in existing owner-occupied units (see Table II-1). Typically, only 8 percent of all owner-occupied units have children 6 years of age or younger, while 21 percent of new units have children in this age group. Thus, if new owner-occupied housing is constructed, such units are likely to be occupied by families with children. The average number of occupants in new owner-occupied housing is 14 percent higher than in all owner-occupied units. Not only are rental units less likely to have children compared to owner-occupied housing, but also the probability of having children under 18 actually declines in new rental units compared to older units. This explains why the number of occupants in new rental units is slightly below the level of older units.

2. <u>Economic Characteristics</u>. Residents of new owner-occupied housing have somewhat higher incomes and purchase more expensive units than residents of older housing (see Table II-3). This gap increased between 1973 and 1974, when new house values increased by 15 percent and incomes of new housing purchasers increased only 13 percent. The median value of new owner-occupied units is more than 33 percent higher than the average value of the older stock, while incomes are only 8 percent higher. The income gap between those renting and owning housing units increased between 1973 and 1974. The pattern differs among renters of new units. These residents have an income which is 32 percent above the average of all residents of

rental units, while their rent is only 26 percent higher. Owners allocate a larger percentage of their income for housing compared to renters. This expenditure gap is reduced if personal income tax offsets available to owners are calculated.

These characteristics indicated that new housing is typically more expensive to purchase or to rent than the existing housing stock. They further suggest that new housing will not meet the housing needs of residents whose incomes are at or below the community median.

3. Housing Characteristics. Housing units (both for sale and rent) built since 1970 have fewer rooms than older units (see Table II-3), a reversal of the pattern found between 1950 and 1970, when the size of the average new dwelling unit for sale increased. The data also show that 92 percent of owner-occupied housing (excluding mobile homes) are detached or attached single units. What may be surprising is that mobile homes account for 18 percent of all new owner-occupied housing. If one excludes households in mobile homes, the median income of owner-occupied units increases substantially above the values shown Table II-4.

C. RELATIONSHIP BETWEEN HOUSEHOLD CHARACTERISTICS AND HOUSING DEMAND 1970 AND 1974

In 1974, the median income of households purchasing housing was $13,800. The median value of a new housing unit was $36,300, or roughly 2.6 times current income. Mortgage loans represented 74.7 percent of the housing unit purchase price. The average downpayment for housing was $9,810 and the average mortgage was $27,120, twice the median 1974 income. These ratios are consistent with mortgage practices by lending institutions. A general rule is that if a new housing unit sells for $50,000, households in

TABLE II-3. U.S. HOUSING UNIT CHARACTERISTICS, 1973

| | OWNER-OCCUPIED | | RENTAL-OCCUPIED | |
|---|---|---|---|---|
| | All Housing | New Housing | All Housing | New Housing |
| Median Number of Rooms | 5.7 | 5.3 | 4.0 | 3.8 |
| 1 Unit Detached (%) | 84 | 67 a/ | 28 | 11 a/ |
| 2 to 4 Units (%) | 5 | 3 | 27 | 17 |
| 5 or More Units (%) | 1 | 3 | 41 | 68 |
| Mobile/Home Trailer (%) | 6 | 18 | 2 | 4 |

SOURCE: U.S., Bureau of the Census, Annual Housing Survey: 1973, part A (July 1975).

a/ Attached and detached one unit housing. Detached units only are not calculated.

the community earning $20,000 or over are eligible to purchase this housing.

The 2.6 to 1 house value-income ratio represents a significant shift since 1970. As Table II-4 indicates, the median value of owner-occupied housing increased by 59 percent between 1970 and 1974, while the income of residents increased only 32 percent. Thus, homeowners during 1974 and 1975 spent a larger share of their income on housing than those purchasing housing in prior years. This was caused more by a rapid increase in the value of the existing housing stock and the cost of construction between 1970 and 1974 than by increases in personal income.

A similar but less intensive shift occurred in rental housing. Between 1970 and 1974, median rent payments increased by 37 percent, while the median income of renters increased only 22 percent. Monthly gross rent for all rental units as a percentage of income rose from 19 to 23 percent.[19] Households moving into new apartments and other rental units in 1973 allocated 22 percent of their income for housing, or slightly less than those living in older units. In fact, households allocated an even higher percentage of disposable income during 1974 and 1975 than in 1970, more than these percentages would suggest, since the proportion of gross income allocated for local and state taxes in each income category has risen, reducing disposable income.

These changes, which may be only temporary, illustrate the danger of assuming an arbitrary percentage of income should be allocated for housing and of estimating economic and noneconomic demand on the basis of this

19. As income of a household rises, the demand for owner-occupied housing rises faster than for rental units. For review of research, see Frank deLeeuw, The Demand for Housing.

TABLE II-4 CHANGES IN U.S. HOUSING CHARACTERISTICS, 1970-74

## OWNER-OCCUPIED HOUSING

| | MEDIAN VALUE 1970 | 1974 | PERCENT CHANGE | MEDIAN INCOME 1969 | 1973 | PERCENT CHANGE | MEDIAN NUMBER OF PERSONS 1970 | 1974 | PERCENT CHANGE |
|---|---|---|---|---|---|---|---|---|---|
| All Housing | $17,000 | $27,200 | 59.2 | $9,700 | $12,800 | 31.9 | 3.0 | 2.8 | -6.7 |
| New Housing | N/A | 36,300 | N/A | N/A | 13,800 | N/A | N/A | 3.3 | N/A |
| Difference (%) | --- | 33.5 | --- | --- | N/A | --- | --- | 17.9 | --- |

## RENTAL-OCCUPIED UNITS

| | MEDIAN RENT a/ 1970 | 1974 | PERCENT CHANGE | MEDIAN INCOME 1969 | 1973 | PERCENT CHANGE | MEDIAN NUMBER OF PERSONS 1970 | 1974 | PERCENT CHANGE |
|---|---|---|---|---|---|---|---|---|---|
| All Rental Units | $108 | $148 | 37.0 | $6,300 | $7,700 | 22.2 | 2.3 | 2.1 | -8.7 |
| New Rental Units | N/A | 186 | --- | N/A | 10,200 | --- | N/A | 2.0 | --- |
| Difference (%) | --- | 25.6 | --- | --- | 32.4 | --- | --- | -4.8 | --- |

SOURCE: U.S., Bureau of the Census, Annual Housing Survey: 1974, part A, advance report (March 1976).
a/ Includes subsidized housing.

percentage.[20] A study based on data gathered in the late 1960s concluded that 20 percent of gross income is the highest rent a family with below average income can afford.[21] On the basis of more recent data, it would appear that 22 to 25 percent is more representative of actual outlays.

More than one-third of all homeowners buy homes costing three or more times their current gross income. In many cases, the homeowners are required to make substantial downpayments to qualify for mortgages. While this number may appear unreasonably high, many families consider homeownership a form of savings in an inflationary period, and invest in housing which exceeds their basic needs. In addition, the tax benefits for homeowners, particularly for households earning $20,000 or more, are substantial. Since a 6 percent annual inflation rate is projected for the coming years, housing allocations are not expected to change in the corresponding period.

A recently completed study examined the relationship between homeownership and income, race, and household age.[22] Findings produced by this study were consistent with data from the Annual Housing Survey and showed that the income elasticity for homeownership is greatest as income rises between $4,000 and $10,000. The homeownership rate is highest among husband-wife families between the ages of 45 and 65, while the rate among primary individuals is only 31 percent.[23] However, as income rises, the youngest families are the most likely to seek homeownership.

---

20. No doubt, the Los Angeles study cited previously, if updated to re-reflect 1973 data, would find a third or more of its affluent residents "paying too much" for housing.

21. The Report of the President's Committee on Urban Housing, vol. I (Washington, D.C.: U.S. Government Printing Office, 1967).

Raymond J. Struyk and Sue A. Marshall, "Income and Homeownership," The Review of Economics and Statistics (February 1975). The study uses 1970 statistics.

23. Average income of those 45-65 years of age is $16,616 compared to $15,510 for those 30-44 years of age and $11,412 for those under the age of 30.

D.  ESTIMATING DEMAND-- A NUMERICAL EXAMPLE

The following example illustrates an inexpensive method for estimating
the relationship between proposed new residential development and the share
of local population forming a potential market for this housing.

A local planning office is asked to evaluate the likely number of
local residents who may buy or rent housing in a proposed Planned Unit
Development (PUD).  Housing by type, selling price, and monthly rent is
shown in the following tabulation:

| Unit Type | Selling Price/Monthly Rent |
|---|---|
| 1-2 Bedroom Garden Apartments | $175, One Bedroom; $225, Two Bedroom |
| 2-3 Bedroom Townhouse Units for Rent | $260, Two Bedroom; $300, Three Bedroom |
| 3 Bedroom, 3 + Den Townhouses for Sale | $36,000 to $45,000 |
| 3-5 Bedroom Detached Units for Sale | $48,000, 3 Bedroom; $57,000, 4 Bedroom; $65,000, 5 Bedroom. |

What proportion of community residents can afford to purchase or rent
these units?  To estimate the effective demand, develop criteria on the
share of income that residents can allocate for housing (based on the discussion in the previous sections of this chapter).  The following guidelines
assume that a household has savings for 25 percent cash downpayment.  For
FHA mortgages, a 10 percent downpayment would require higher ratios.

Category A - Elderly 1-2 person, or other one person households:  33
percent of income for rent; 3 times annual income to purchase non-FHA housing.

Category B - 2-3 person household, or one dependent child:  30 percent
of income for rent; 2.75 times annual income to purchase non-FHA housing.

Category C - 4 or more person household; 25 percent of income for rent;
2.5 times income to purchase non-FHA housing.

Table  II-5 changes these guidelines to minimum income requirements for

TABLE II-5. MINIMUM INCOME REQUIREMENTS BY UNIT TYPE

| | Rent/House Value | Minimum Income Requirements | | |
| --- | --- | --- | --- | --- |
| | | A | B | C |
| Garden Apartment | | | | |
| 1 Bedroom | $ 175 | $ 6,300 | $ 6,930 | N/A a/ |
| 2 Bedroom | 225 | 8,100 | 9,000 | $10,800 |
| Townhouse | | | | |
| 2 Bedroom | 260 | 9,360 | 10,300 | 12,480 |
| 3 Bedroom | 300 | 10,800 | 12,000 | 14,400 |
| 3 Bedroom | 36,000 | 12,000 | 13,100 | 14,000 |
| 4 Bedroom | 45,000 | 15,000 | 16,350 | 18,000 |
| Detached | | | | |
| 4 Bedroom | 57,000 | 19,000 | 20,730 | 22,800 |
| 5 Bedroom | 65,000 | 21,667 | 23,636 | 26,000 |

a/
Does not meet adequate housing standards, since households with four or more persons require two or more bedrooms. The Los Angeles Housing Authority uses the following criteria: one bedroom, maximum two occupants; two bedroom, four occupants; three bedrooms, six occupants.

housing shown in Table II-2.   The distribution of household income, based on the 1973 national pattern, is shown in Table  II-6.

As demonstrated in this example, more than one-third of all households, with the exception of the elderly, could not afford to rent housing in the prototype development if housing prices and income distribution in the "typical" community were close to the 1973 national average.  At the same time, more than one-half of all households could not afford to buy housing in the development.  About 30 percent of the households could buy or rent any of the housing except the most expensive detached unit model.

E.   PROPORTION OF COMMUNITY RESIDENTS LIKELY TO PURCHASE NEW HOUSING

Calculating the proportion of the community population that can afford to buy or rent new units provides estimates of the potential economic demand and thus represents a maximum number.  In addition to local residents, inmigrants to the region and residents of nearby communities may also buy or rent new units.  Since inmigrants generally have higher incomes than the base population, these households would be expected to purchase or rent a substantial number of new units, particularly in rapidly growing areas. In addition, inmigrants are likely to be members of those age groups with the highest elasticity  of homeownership. Finally, unlike present residents, inmigrants must acquire housing.

This view is supported by data which show that one-third of all households moving into owner-occupied housing in 1974 purchased units built between 1970 and 1973, although only 10 percent of the total housing stock was built in this three-year period.[24]   The data also show that more than half of those moving into owner-occupied housing resided outside the SMSA in which the present unit is located.  About 20 percent of renters move into

24. U.S.,Bureau of the Census, Annual Housing Survey, part D, (November 1975).

TABLE II-6. INCOME DISTRIBUTION AND HOUSING DEMAND, 1973

| Income Category | Percentage [a] | HOUSING IN NEW DEVELOPMENT | |
| | | Rental | Purchase |
| --- | --- | --- | --- |
| Under $4,000 | 17.5 | None | None |
| $4,000-$7,000 | 15.4 | 1 Bedroom for Elderly Only | None |
| $7,000-$10,000 | 14.6 | Elderly, 1-2 Person Households Only | None |
| $10,000-$15,000 | 22.6 | All Units | 3 Bedroom Townhouse, No Detached Units |
| $15,000-$25,000 | 22.1 | All Units | All Except 5 Bedroom Detached |
| $25,000 and Over | 7.8 | All Units | All Units |
| Median | $10,500 | Elderly, 1-2 Person, 2 Bedroom | None |

a/  The distribution represents the national income division
during 1973 based on data from the U.S. Bureau of the Census.

units three years old or newer.  These newer units comprise about 10 percent of the total housing stock.

Factors affecting the likely local resident share of the market include the number of units taken out of stock within a year, housing vacancy rates, changes in personal income, the type of unit presently occupied, the size (both total population and spatial) of the community, and size of the metropolitan area.  For example, in jurisdictions such as Montgomery County, Maryland, or Fairfax County, Virginia, both of which incorporate more than 400 square miles with populations in excess of 550,000, the number of former county residents who purchase new housing is likely to be high.  In small jurisdictions that are part of a large metropolitan area, occupancy by local residents may be only 10 percent.

Sternlieb's analysis is one of the few studies to identify previous place of residence by type of housing.[25]  By examining a number of new developments in New Jersey, Sternlieb found that only 8 percent of townhouse residents and 11 percent of highrise apartment residents previously lived in the same community.[26]  However, 21 percent of those residing in single family homes and garden apartments were previously community residents. The proportion of residents previously living outside New Jersey was 37 percent, reflecting New Jersey's role as a "bedroom state" for the New York and Philadelphia metropolitan areas.  This is probably a higher out of state percentage than for other states.

---

25.  George Sternlieb, Housing Development and Municipal Costs, Rutgers University, Center for Urban Policy Research, 1973.

26.  The population of communities examined varied from a few thousand to over fifty thousand.

Data on the proportion of all residents who previously lived in the community, metropolitan area, or state are available at the census tract level for all SMSAs for 1970.  However, these data do not distinguish between occupants of new and older housing, although data on the proportion of units built in recent years in each census tract are available.  Thus, it is possible to estimate the proportion of households in those census tracts comprised primarily of new units by determining the households' previous residence.

The New Jersey findings, fragmentary data from census tracts in the Washington, D.C., SMSA, and the Annual Housing Survey data support the view that the probability of local residents' occupying a large share of new housing is low.

# IV.  ANALYTIC TOOLS FOR ESTIMATING HOUSING NEEDS

## A.  FACTORS AFFECTING DEMAND AND SUPPLY

The usefulness of analytic methods as predictive tools depends on how well factors influencing the demand and supply of housing can be identified and on how well the impact of these factors can be assessed.

Future housing demand depends on changes in the characteristics of the base population and the level of inmigration or outmigration.  Various Census Bureau publications provide data for estimating the number of new households likely to be formed, based on the current demographic profile of the population.  However, net migration, even at the regional level, is more difficult to forecast.  The typical approach is to assume the continuation of historical patterns.  However, major directional shifts in migration at the local, regional, and state levels have taken place during the past decade, illustrating the weakness of this assumption, even over a short time period.  For example, both Denver and Los Angeles experienced substantial inmigration during the 1960s, followed by rapid outmigration in the 1970s.

Estimating the future supply of housing units is also difficult.  The supply is affected by the addition of new housing, the removal of existing housing by demolition or conversion to nonhousing use, the rehabilitation of substandard units, and the addition of larger units by conversion.  The extent of these activities depends on several exogenous factors, including federal policies, interest rates, and local land use regulations.  Since both private and public activities affect the supply of housing, it is unlikely that any workable model will reliably predict housing supply in a region. However, well designed analytic models can indicate the degree to which changes in interest rates, for example, affect the level of new construction.

B. THE USE OF HOUSING MODELS

Housing typically forms a component, or submodel, of general land use models. (see Part II). The general structure of housing submodels is discussed in a publication dealing with residential location patterns.[27] Most of these models use household characteristics to determine the type of housing unit a family is most likely to buy or rent. The models vary in complexity, ranging from those using four or five combinations of household characteristics and housing units to one allocating households to each of 72 different socioeconomic classes among 44 residential zones and 27 types of housing. However, even the more complex models do not take into account such factors as differences in relative prices of various housing types within a metropolitan area attributable to local housing policies, and the cost of land.

This report has focused on _inexpensive_ methods to estimate housing demand. Unfortunately, none of the models examined fits this category in application. In addition, some of the basic assumptions that "drive" these models are questionable. For example, a major objective of the City of Los Angeles study[28] was to determine the housing "gap." This was defined for the city on the basis of two criteria: (1) rent/income ratios greater than 25 percent, and (2) overcrowding (defined as more than one person per

27. Franklin J. James and James W. Wright, _Economic Growth and Residential Patterns_ (New Brunswick: Rutgers University, 1972).

28. _Los Angeles Housing Model_, op. cit.

room regardless of outlay for housing). Data from the 1970 Census were applied at the census tract level to estimate how many households had an "unmet housing need" forming the gap. The study concluded that the problem is not housing per se but insufficient income. Presumably, if people had higher income they would spend less on housing.[29] The model then estimated the cost of housing allowances to ameliorate the housing problem, i.e., to close the gap to a point where no household would spend more than 25 percent of its income for housing, be crowded, or live in poor quality housing.

The use of this methodology (also applied in San Francisco and other cities) to estimate the impact of new housing on meeting housing needs is questionable. For example, the model does not test the impact of new housing on the "gap." In the absence of new housing, a subsidy policy would raise the cost of existing rental (and other) units, offsetting the objective of the policy at considerable public expense. The major weaknesses of the model are that the income-to-rent ratios appear arbitrary and that the effects of new housing are not explicitly evaluated.

San Francisco developed a complex housing model in the 1960s to predict the potential effects of various community housing policies on the city's housing stock.[30] Households were grouped into the following categories: no children, children, size, race, and income. One objective of the model was to predict new housing construction by type. While the model successfully predicted total _investment_, projections of new housing estimates by type of structure did not adequately reflect actual construction. The San Francisco

29. This view contradicts studies which show that housing is income-elastic. That is, as income rises, outlays for housing increase more rapidly than incomes.
30. Arthur D. Little, Inc., _Model of San Francisco Housing Market_, Technical Report 8, (January 1966).

model, never fully operational, is extremely complex, and perhaps a good example of the technical difficulties and high costs of attempting to use sophisticated simulation techniques to estimate housing supply and demand. This approach is <u>not</u> recommended for use by other communities.

One early land use model applied by the staff of the Southeastern Wisconsin regional planning group determines regional housing demand by assigning a type of house to each of 16 different types of households.[31] The amount of housing each type is likely to consume is determined exogenously (outside the model) by estimating inmigration, family formation rates, and relocation rates. A linear programming routine assigns numerous tracks for the appropriate number of housing units by minimizing land development costs. A more important determinant of housing type by location, the price of land, is not considered. Households are allocated to new housing on the basis of accessibility to employment and shopping. Since the model's documentation is inadequate, its usefulness is difficult to assess.

Research undertaken at The Urban Institute has examined the effects of housing policies on housing supply and demand. Several models have been developed as part of this research, and the results have been discussed in several Institute Reports.[32] While these models have proved to be a useful policy tool at the <u>regional</u> or metropolitan level, they are not designed for local application.

While most models concentrate on estimating the demand for housing, the supply of new housing at a particular location is determined, in most

31. Wisconsin, Southeastern Regional Planning Commission, <u>Technical Reports 3, 5, and 8</u> (1966 and 1968).
32. See, for example, Frank deLeeuw et al., <u>The Market Effects of Housing Policies</u> (Washington, D.C.: The Urban Institute, October 1974).

instances, by private developer decision.  This aspect of housing supply has been examined by Kaiser.[33]

A review of formal models and supporting studies indicates that the models' usefulness is limited to estimating housing supply and its likely location at the regional level.  From the local perspective, the approach outlined earlier, despite its many limitations, appears more cost-effective in application than the computer-assisted analytic tools discussed in this section.

---

33.  Edward Kaiser, "Locational Decision Factors in a Producer Model of Residential Development," Land Economics, (1968).

# V.   FINDINGS AND RECOMMENDATIONS

Since the availability of housing is one of the major issues at the local level, an understanding of the supply and demand relationships between proposed new housing, existing housing, and needs of community residents is an important part in any impact analysis.

This report has shown that a community can estimate the impact of new residential development, including ways in which the existing housing supply will be affected and the proportion of local households forming the potential market for new housing. The report has emphasized that housing must be examined from both the local and regional perspective, since housing markets extend beyond the political boundaries of any local government.

Also discussed were methods for estimating local household economic and demographic characteristics. These two items are crucial in examining the short-term effects of new housing on the housing preferences of local residents.

On the basis of data from recent housing surveys, the report has discussed shifts in the relationship between household characteristics and owner-occupied as well as rental housing. These changes emphasize the importance of using only the most current information. Basic procedures to link household characteristics to effective and noneffective housing demand were also illustrated.

These procedures should be applied in the absence of local surveys to estimate the likely housing impact of individual developments. Determining aggregate community and regional housing supply and demand relationships requires the use of complex computer-based models, the operation of which is beyond the capabilities of most jurisdictions. Housing models are still in the developmental stage. Therefore, the outlay of resources required for their use is difficult to justify, particularly at the local level. In the absence of access to models that can be easily adapted for use at the municipal level, the methods discussed in this report can be used to project the incremental impact of new residential housing.

PART III—IMPACT OF DEVELOPMENT ON REAL PROPERTY VALUE

# I.  INTRODUCTION AND BACKGROUND

## A.  REAL PROPERTY AS A COMPONENT OF WEALTH

Real property represents the dominant share of all personal tangible assets and more than one-third of all personal wealth in the nation.  The other major component of personal wealth is made up of cash, stocks, and bonds. New developments primarily affect the real property components of wealth, although the value of intangible assets can be affected indirectly by growth. Among middle income households residing in owner-occupied housing, about half of total personal wealth is in the form of real estate.  Wealth in areas experiencing population growth and expanding economies, including Texas and the southeast region, is concentrated heavily in real estate(less prevalent in states with generally stagnant economies).  This is attributable to the role of agricultural land in the economy of these areas and anticipation of future growth.

While new developments can indirectly affect other components of wealth, this report focuses on the effects of development on the value of land and improvements.

## B.  RELATIONSHIP BETWEEN CHANGES IN PROPERTY VALUES AND IMPACT EVALUATION

If new residential or nonresidential construction changes the value of existing property, it also affects the _wealth_ of property owners.  Such changes, likely as new employment opportunities increase inmigration, can have a large _fiscal_ impact on a community.  Changes in property value, when reflected in higher or lower costs of housing, have a social effect, particularly on low-income residents who allocate a substantial share of their money income to shelter.

C. COMMUNITY INTERESTS AND OBJECTIVES

The impact of development on property value is of interest to communities for one or more of the following reasons:

1. A reduction in property value resulting from adverse effects of new development is politically undesirable, since owner-occupied housing residents react sharply to such a possibility. On the other hand, the group favorably views a potential increase in property value, although the higher housing costs that result are disadvantageous to prospective residents.

2. A change in the value of the current housing stock and other real property will be reflected in the level of property tax receipts when property is reassessed. This, in turn, can affect the community's fiscal position.

3. A general increase in land value means that the public sector must spend more to purchase rights of way, school sites, and other facilities.

If a community decides to examine property value changes, the following elements should be incorporated into the analysis:

1. Impact of new development on land and property values very near the new development and in the community;

2. Key factors that caused observed changes, if any, in property values;

3. Economic and social implications of such changes on the community.

D. REAL PROPERTY--LAND AND IMPROVEMENTS

Examinations of the value of real property must distinguish between unimproved and improved land (i.e., land with structures). Improved land can be further divided into a land component and structures on the land. The value of land has been estimated at between 29 and 38 percent of all taxable real estate in 1960. It is reasonable to assume, on the basis of past trends, that by 1976 the land share of all real property has increased to between 34 to 35 percent.

This rise over time is attributable to the fact that land is not reproducible. As real income rises, the demand for land-intensive housing, recreation, and other activities increases. With the population growing at an average annual rate of 1 percent, the _per capita_ quantity of unimproved land, particularly near urban areas, is further reduced.[1] Thus, land values generally increase more rapidly than other investments that can be reproduced or extracted.

In theory, the value of land can be distinguished from improvements on the land. Presumably, the value of land would be its highest and best use independent of any structures.[2] While many communities require assessors to distinguish between the two components for tax purposes, the distinction is often arbitrary. In general, structures are depreciated in value (in real dollars) to reflect a reduction in their economic life. Thus, when the selling price of a housing unit in a neighborhood increases, the assessor "credits" most of the appreciation to the land on the assumption that this increase is attributable to amenities which accrue to the land rather than the structure.[3] This allocation has little pratical meaning, since the selling price of similar units rather than the allocation between land and improvements determines the assessed value of detached housing. In addition, the same tax rate applies to land and improvements, although farm property is an exception to this rule in some states.

1. During the 1960s, population growth nationally exceeded the 1 percent annual level. Between 1970 and 1975, growth averaged 0.9 percent each year.
2. The cost of demolition needs to be subtracted to estimate the net value of land.
3. During an inflationary period, the value of the structure may also increase if the added cost of reproducing a similar dwelling unit more than offsets the physical

E.  <u>PUBLIC AND PRIVATE INVESTMENT</u>

Public investment, particularly transportation routes, water mains, and sewer lines, has a significant positive effect on land value.  In the absence of such investments, the development potential of land is limited to very low density housing accessible by private roads.  Some public investments, however, such as airports, sewage treatment plants, gravel pits, and other environmentally or aesthetically unattractive facilities, can adversely affect property values.  Private investment, in the form of new industrial and commercial facilities, can also have an adverse effect on nearby land. The role of the public sector in influencing property value changes is typically greater than private investment activities.

# II. MAJOR DETERMINANTS OF LAND VALUE

## A. AMENITIES AND ACCESSIBILITY

This section explores factors that affect land values. Included are amenities, accessibility, and zoning regulations.

1. Residential Use. The value of land at a particular site, especially residential land, is a function of several variables, including accessibility, neighborhood and community amenities, topography, income of residents, and the amount of nearby developable open spaces.[4] Unless transportation facilities are involved, new developments will have only a marginal immediate impact on accessibility to an area. In the short run, accessibility can be decreased (in terms of time required to reach a destination) if congestion is caused by the addition of housing or other activities. This may be offset, in the long run, by the greater population concentration, which can result in road or mass transit improvements in the vicinity of growth.

The impact of new development on amenities in an area can also be substantial. If an area is believed to possess better amenities in terms of natural features (lakes, views from heights), social characteristics (affluent households, private clubs), or public facilities (good schools, high level of public safety), equally accessible land in this area will have a substantially higher value. Population growth can increase or decrease any of the perceived amenities. Thus, new residential development can reduce an area's

---

4. The minimum value of land is generally its agricultural potential which, as in the case of an orange grove, can be substantial. However, urbanization pressures frequently result in demand for residential use which raises the price above its agricultural value, including use as orange groves, as is evident in the reduction of citrus production near urban centers in both California and Florida.

social exclusiveness and the quality of its public services, at least in the short run. However, since the development process reduces the amount of open land available for future development, it will tend to offset potentially adverse fiscal effects by increasing both the value of and the taxes derived from the remaining undeveloped land.

2. <u>Nonresidential Uses</u>. Nonresidential property and high density residential property values are more sensitive to differences in accessibility than are low density residential housing values. Land zoned for commercial use, for example, is extremely valuable if located near intersections of major road networks or in urbanized areas. Almost all major shopping centers are located near highway intersections or near exits of major highways so that the greatest number of potential shoppers can reach the center is 20, 30, or 40 minutes. Neighborhood amenities have only minimal effects on the value of commercial or industrial property, since occupants use few services other than utilities and police and fire protection at the site. While retail outlets catering to higher income households locate near affluent neighborhoods, this pattern is attributable to market accessibility rather than to greater neighborhood amenities.

Industrial property is generally most valuable if located near major transportation facilities such as highways, railroads, and, to a lesser extent, airports. However, such factors as accessibility to the type of housing employees would likely occupy and the location of complementary industries also influence land values.

B. <u>ANTICIPATION OF FURTHER GROWTH</u>

A new development is most likely to have its greatest effect on the value of real property located close to the project. A large shopping center will have little measurable effect on property values four to five miles from its

location.  However, the value of property adjoining the center may change.
Thus additional growth can cause residential structures to drop in value because of additional noise, pollution, lights, and traffic congestion nearby.
If additional growth is not anticipated nearby, property values can become
depressed.  Housing a mile or so away may become somewhat more valuable since
accessibility to shopping and employment is improved without congestion and
other adverse effects.  However, if the new shopping center is likely to
attract complementary retail stores and office space, the land component of
property immediately adjacent will increase.  While the improvement component
of a land parcel will decrease in value due to adverse effects, the land component can increase in value so much that housing units will be demolished
if zoning  to allow commercial development can be easily obtained.

Thus, two interrelated factors can increase the value of land near a
privately sponsored project such as a shopping center, or near a public
investment such as a transit station on a mass transit line.  Without anticipated additional growth, improved accessibility to employment centers, shopping, or other areas connected by the transit network will increase the value
of improved property near a transportation station if negative externalities
(congestion, noise) are more than offset by the benefits accruing from locational advantages gained by accessibility.  If further growth is expected--
a more typical situation--the value of unimproved land will increase.  The
component of land value attributable to future growth represents anticipated
rents.[5]

---

5.  Those rents are defined as returns above the cost of production
attributable to the natural limitations in the supply of land.  For conceptual
framework, see William Alonso, Location and Land Use Toward a General Theory
of Land Rent (Cambridge, Mass.: Harvard University Press, 1964).

From the <u>community</u> or <u>regional</u> perspective, however, the increase in the value of land near the new development will be offset, partially or fully, by reduced land values in other parts of the region, unless economic activity in the total region increases as a result of a private or public investment. That is, a new shopping center or road interchange merely <u>shifts</u> economic activity from one area to another with little or no net gain. Thus, while property owners near the site can benefit substantially, all other owners in the region will experience a minor or perhaps immeasurably small loss. If these shifts are concentrated within one community in the region, considerable fiscal effects can result.

## C. <u>ZONING</u>

More than 90 percent of cities with 5,000 or more residents, and all large cities except Houston, have some form of zoning based on the concept of "external diseconomies." This concept means that since some land uses such as glue factories would reduce the value of nearby property, the exclusion through zoning of such facilities will preserve property values. Since zoning excludes "adverse" types of development from an area, one result can be higher values for existing property than would be the case if there were no land use controls.[6] Zoning has only a marginal effect on the price of land for low density development, since most land    suburban jurisdictions is placed in this category. One objective of blanket low density zoning (called "exclusionary zoning" or "fiscal zoning"), which prohibits high density residential construction is to preserve the property values of de-tached housing by ensuring that few, if any, apartments are built.[7]

---

6. Similarly, zoning can also result in an aggregate reduction in property value.

7. For a discussion of fiscal zoning and related issues, see James W. Hughes, ed. <u>New Dimensions in Urban Planning - Growth Controls</u>, Rutgers University, Center for Urban Policy Research, (1974).

In such communities, land available through zoning variances for high density residential construction is more valuable than would be the case in the absence of blanket zoning.

In most communities, zoning is likely to have at least a short-term effect on the selling price of land designated for more intensive use. The importance of zoning is generally linked to the ease with which the zoning can be changed, which frequently involves only a transaction cost. As noted by Neutze in a case study of apartment construction in a suburban county, "the legal cost of a good zoning lawyer could possibly be regarded as the cost of getting rezoning."[8] In other areas, however, costs are higher. For example, strong citizen political opposition can result is expensive residential housing is located near an area for which a rezoning request has been made to expand a newly built industrial facility. If such opposition is likely, current property values would include the level of uncertainty associated with rezoning due to this opposition.[9]

The quantity of land already zoned for intensive use also influences the value of land near large projects. Scarcity of such nearby land creates an upward price pressure, whereas substantial acreage relatively close, but not necessarily adjacent, to a new project zoned for intensive use will have a dampening effect.

While it is easy to show that land zoned for commercial, industrial, and high density residential use is more valuable than land zoned for low density residential use, factors other than zoning, particularly accessibility, must

---

8. Max Neutze, The Suburban Apartment Boom (Baltimore, Md.: Johns Hopkins Press, 1968). Neutze was referring to the situation at one point in time.
    9. If local officials declare an area as one which cannot be rezoned, the value of the land will reflect the likelihood that the decision will be reversed later.

be considered.  For example, land zoned for intensive use is closer to major

transportation facilities than land zoned for less intensive use.  The amount

of land zoned for intensive use  also influences the value of commercial

and industrial land.[10]

---

10. For variations in the value of land zoned by type and the effects
of location and quantity of vacant land, see Thomas Muller, "Implicit Grants
to Property Owners at the Local Level."  In Redistribution to the Rich and the
Poor, edited by Kenneth Boulding and Martin Pfaff, Wadsworth Publishing
Company, 1972.

## III. IMPACT OF DEVELOPMENT
## ON PROPERTY VALUES—METHODS AND EFFECTS

This section discusses methods available to planners and others for estimating the impact of new development on the value of property. Two general approaches are discussed, although neither may provide useful results. Findings based on empirical results are noted, although these results may not be transferable, since each land use site has one or more unique characteristics.

### A. METHODS OF ANALYSIS

1. _Comparative Approach_. The impact of new development on property values can be estimated by a number of approaches. One method is to match neighborhoods or areas with all but one similar characteristic. For example, the value of similar detached housing in two developments, one near an industrial facility and high density housing area and the other contiguous to other detached housing units, can be compared. Differences found in the two developments would then be attributed to the perception of benefits to the neighborhood from nearby land uses. This comparative approach is relatively simple to apply but has one major drawback--it is very hard to identify two areas that are similar in all ways except one, since developments with similar characteristics typically vary in matters like distance from employment centers, major roads, or schools.

Nonetheless, this comparative technique has been applied to determine the impact of public housing on surrounding land values in St. Louis.[11] The objective was to determine whether the site value of a neighborhood increases

_____
11.  Hugh O. Nourse, "The Effect of Public Housing on Property Values in St. Louis," _Land Economics_, (Madison, Wisconsin - November 1963).

if public housing is built. The study concludes that there is no evidence that new public housing located in low-income areas increases the value of surrounding property. In fact, not surprisingly the opposite was found--prices in some cases decreased.

The comparative approach is also used in transportation studies; land values near highway interchanges or mass transit stations are compared to values in similar areas without such transportation facilities. One study in Chicago paired 18 test and control areas and concluded that land values increased more rapidly along the new highway corridor than in "control" areas where no such new development occurred.[12] Industrial property value increased the most (18 percent); while residential property value increased the least (9 percent).

Not surprisingly, transportation studies usually find that the value of land near new transportation facilities is higher than for other areas. These results, in turn, are frequently cited as evidence of benefits which accrue from such public investments.[13]

Similar techniques can be applied to compare adjacent land and housing values before and after the construction of a major facility, such as a shopping center. Changes in property value at these sites are compared with overall changes in value within the community. Differences are then presumably attributable to the new development.

---

12. Jay S. Goblen, "Land Values in Chicago Before and After Expressway Construction," Chicago Area Transportation Study (October 1961).

13. These studies frequently ignore the aggregate property value impact of these public investments. As noted previously, unless the new facilities increase the demand for nonresidential land use, increases in value near transit stations may be offset by reductions in value in other areas. For a critique of transportation studies dealing with property values, see Charles River Associates, Measurements of the Effects of Transportation Changes (July 1972).

2. <u>Regression Techniques</u>. A commonly applied approach, favored by researchers, is the use of regression techniques to examine change in land value. Certain variables such as distance to major transportation arteries, income, and closeness to the central business district (CBD) are included in regression equations as explanatory variables. It is assumed, a priori, that these variables affect property value. The results of the analysis test the relative importance, if any, of each variable in explaining the value of unimproved land or all real property. If certain variable, explain difference in land value which is statistically significant, it is assumed that the addition of these factors near a site, such as improving accessibility to major roads, would change the value of the property. A major advantage of this technique is that "control" areas are not necessary. One drawback is that considerable effort is required to obtain data for identified variables. Also, the set of variables selected explains only 50 to 70 percent of the variation in land value, suggesting that unidentified factors are almost as important.

B. STUDY FINDINGS

1. <u>Effects of Aggregate Development</u>. A comprehensive case study of the Los Angeles area, using regression techniques, examined the relationship between land value and site characteristics such as distance to the CBD.[14] The study concluded that land value changes cannot be attributed to accessibility (such as distance to CBD) unless amenities are taken into account. Thus, two areas equally near the CBD have very different land values. This is not surprising if one examines abandoned housing patterns in the central cities. The value of land in some parts of Newark, New Jersey, for example, is a fraction of the cost in more "exclusive" suburban areas which are also twice

14. Eugene F. Brigham, "The Determinants of Residential Land Values," <u>Land Economics</u> (November 1965).

as far from the New York City or the Newark CBD, although both areas may have the same proportion of New York City or Newark CBD commuters.

Other case studies, including one performed in Raleigh, North Carolina, have also examined residential land values using travel habit surveys and site amenities as inputs to estimate the values.[15] The Raleigh study also used regression analysis to derive its results. These studies show that the demand for amenities is very income-elastic. For every dollar increase in income, demand for additional land increases by a factor of 2.5.

A study of central city land values demonstrates that when census tract housing data are adjusted for income, both land and improvement values per square foot decline at a decreasing rate per mile from the CBD.[16]

The most recent comprehensive analysis of the impact of development by types on the value of existing property was undertaken by Stull, whose conclusions are consistent with general perception.[17] Using data collected for the Boston SMSA at the community level, Stull concluded that the conversion of land from single-family use to other uses will lower average single-family home property values (if employment and taxes are held constant). Specifically, Stull's use of regression techniques led to the conclusion that if 10 percent of a community's land is converted from single-family homes to other uses the average 1960 value will be lowered by $810, or about 5 percent. Stull also found that industrial use has a more adverse impact on single-family homes, than on multiple-family structures. These findings are based on cross-sectional data of aggregate development in each category.

15. R.N. Harris, G. S. Tolley, and C. Harrell, "The Residence Site Choice," Review of Economics and Statistics (May 1968).

16. Harold Brodsky, "Residential Land and Improvement Values in a Central City," Land Economics (August 1970).

17. William J. Stull, An Essay on Externalities, Property Values and Urban Zoning, unpublished doctoral dissertation (Cambridge, Mass.: MIT, Department of Economics, October 1971).

A casual examination of detached housing in urban communities shows that such housing in jurisdictions with a dominance of single-family housing has higher average selling prices than has similar housing in communities where much of the property base is multi-unit housing and industry. Such data, however, may be misleading since the majority of housing in communities dominated by detached units is newer and located on larger lots. Stull's work provides the strongest empirical evidence to date that when other factors are held constant, land use has a substantial impact on the value of detached housing at the community level.

At the metropolitan level, Berry has concluded that per capita land values increase as population increases, up to an SMSA population of about 750,000 to one million.[18] That is, the per capita value of land is higher in an SMSA with 500,000 residents than an SMSA with 100,000 residents. He also found that property values tend to be depressed by manufacturing concentrations and are not surprisingly higher in higher income communities. The importance of low density housing on property values is implicit in the finding that when other variables are held constant, residential property values are higher in dispersed, "urban sprawl" metropolitan areas than in areas with more concentrated residential development.

Although empirical research is limited, there is general agreement that higher income households, particularly those with children, tend to prefer low density, land-intensive housing. The addition of such housing at a neighborhood, community, and perhaps even at the SMSA level increases the value of existing low density units.[19]

18. Brian J.L. Berry et al., Land Use, Urban Form and Environmental Quality, (Chicago: University of Chicago, 1971).

19. In part, this may reflect the closing of other land use options. However, it is unlikely that insufficient land would remain in any area for more intensive land use.

The addition of high density, multi-unit housing, which some find objectionable, is likely to have an adverse effect on the value of detached units in many communities. Because the selling and rental prices of high density units are typically below the prices of detached housing, average community income can be lower.[20] Perhaps more important, homeowners view renters as less "socially desirable" since renters are believed by homeowners to include a high proportion of female-headed households, to be more transient and less interested in community welfare, to cause or be the victims of more crime, and to have a lower socioeconomic status than those residing in detached housing. These views, expressed at rezoning hearings, are frequently based on questionable information. While renters often have lower income, are more likely to have only one parent in residence, and are four times as likely to move, none of these facts per se should automatically reduce the community's "quality of life." Nevertheless, such perceptions by homeowners can have an adverse impact on property values.

Adding small shopping centers that are insulated from residences has an effect probably not adverse, perhaps positive, on aggregate residential property. Industrial facilities, particularly those emitting pollution, noise, or odor, and facilities such as airports have a strong negative effect.[21] However, such facilities are unlikely to locate close to expensive residential developments even without zoning, since homeowners who are usually heavily involved in local political activities would resist such land uses.

---

20. For data on this subject, see Part II of this report. The demand for services, particularly education, is also likely to be lower.
21. The basis for zoning ordinances historically has been to avoid contiguous land uses which have "negative externalities." A number of studies documented the adverse price effect of an airport on nearby residential structures.

If the aggregate demand for new development in a region is fixed, increases in land value at one site will decrease land values in other areas of the region. Thus, the net effect on property value may be minimal. If, however, a development such as a large industrial facility, brings growth to the region, property value changes will not be offset.

2. Effects of Large-Scale Development. Although most developments tend to be small, public interest is concentrated on large-scale public and private development, especially on the potential effects on land values of large-scale development, such as PUD's or "New Towns." A study of such effects in Howard County, Maryland, showed that the building of Columbia, a "New Town," resulted in a one to two mile wide "moat" of low property values around the new town, with nodes of high values in rural parts of the county.[22] The general explanation for this is that "externalities were internalized," i.e., the benefits from the location of Columbia (accessibility, anticipated further growth, amenities) were captured within the area of Columbia by the large quantity of land held for future release as the community grows. The benefits (in terms of higher demand for land) did not spill over to areas adjacent to the community. Presumably, the demand for housing and other land uses is expected to be met from unimproved land within the community boundaries. Persons who prefer low density, rural living in the region but also want to be close to the amenities of the new town increased the value of rural land.

A somewhat different effect seems to have occurred in the area around Disneyworld near Orlando, Florida. Although no comparative empirical studies of land values could be found, local real estate agents as well as aggregate county data indicate that Disneyworld increased land values sharply near the

---

22. Mohammad A. Quadeer, "Local Land Market and a New Town," AIP Journal (March 1974).

development. This is evident by the amount of recent construction, particularly motels and other tourist facilities, on highways leading to Disneyworld. Since the Disney developers purchased an extremely large land area to
internalize the type of demand previously created outside the boundaries of
Disneyland, California,during the 1960s, it would seem that the California
experience would have been avoided.

One factor that accounts for differences between Columbia and Disneyworld is the restrictive land use imposed by Disneyworld management. Although substantial land is available, the owners insist on strict land use
controls, discouraging lower price motels, restaurants, fast-food chains,
and gasoline stations on their property. Since the development itself could
not meet the demand for these services, the demand "spilled over" beyond the
extensive land area the developers owned. Disneyworld also created a demand
for similar or complementary amusement attractions within one or two hours
driving distance. In Columbia, housing and shopping facilities were provided
at various price ranges. This satisfied most demand, and no "new towns" were
triggered.

Large-scale shopping centers also have an agglomeration effect--once
shoppers are drawn to an area, other retail outlets wish to locate nearby.
Since many shopping centers have excluded certain types of stores, such as
discount outlets, the excluded establishment is likely to locate on the
periphery, increasing the value of nearby land, particularly if the land is
already zoned for commercial use. This phenomenon can be observed near
regional shopping centers in the suburbs of large metropolitan areas.

3. Estimating Property Value Changes--State of the Art. The major
conclusion from this review of empirical studies is that while there
is considerable understanding of factors that influence the aggregate

value of urban land, there is little information on the effects of specific developments. The few available studies focus on changes in land value as a result of improvement in transportation in the immediate vicinity of the development. One factor explaining the limited quantity of empirical data is that funds for research have been limited to transportation studies. Additional funds, however, would not diminish many of the existing technical problems. For example, it is virtually impossible, in a dynamic urban area, to administer "clean" controlled experiments that compare changes in two or more areas. Equally important, the timing of data collection is a problem. Land values may change several years before actual construction takes place, presumably because "insiders" know of an impending decision to build a shopping center or road at a specific site.

The most significant limitation is that most studies examine only changes in land areas adjacent or close to the development. As noted previously, increases in property value near a project are probably offset by decreases elsewhere in the community or region unless aggregate regional demand for land changes as a result of a project. For example, if the BART mass transit system changes the competitive advantages of the region and produces additional inmigration or outmigration, property value changes near stations would not be offset fully by changes in the rest of the region. However, there is little if any empirical data on regionwide changes, which must take into account such factors as reduced disposable income resulting from the higher local taxes needed to pay for public projects. Thus, land use planning models do not link land prices and the allocation of land to various uses. In these models, the supply and demand for land do not depend on land prices.[23]

---

23.   See, for example, Ira S. Lowry, A Model of a Metropolis (Santa Monica: The Rand Corporation, 1964).

4. <u>The Role of Local Government</u>. Given the limited nature of most land use planning models, is it useful for local government to try to analyze land values? In the introductory comments to this section, several areas of interest were noted. One was public opposition to development believed to have a negative effect on property value. In this instance, past experience can be used to determine if there were such efforts. This approach compares land values in two areas through the following steps:

1. Identify all improved and, separately, unimproved parcels within a radius of one-half mile from the site;

2. Obtain the selling price and assessment history (ten years or more) of each parcel from local records on property transactions and assessments;

3. Select a control site with similar characteristics (including accessibility to housing, shopping, employment, topography, distance to CBD, zoning, and utilities);

4. Repeat steps (1) and (2) for control site.

If many representative parcels have been sold, a meaningful comparison is more likely. If only assessment data are used, the results may be inconclusive, for unimproved land is usually underassessed relative to improved property.

If there are infrequent sales, assessors use their own judgment in estimating the "reasonable" worth for such land. They then apply this value to unimproved land over a large area, ignoring other site-specific factors. Data on recent sales are therefore better than data on values <u>based on assessed to market value conversion</u>. However, the author's experience indicates that if 20 or so parcels near each other are examined, some parcels will have been owned by the same owner for perhaps 50 or more years, while the most recent sale dates of the other parcels will range from six months to ten years. This time variance and infrequent reassessment make it difficult to establish sale prices on a current value base. Thus, it is often frustrating if not impossible to measure land values with a comparative approach. Another problem, noted previously, is finding a control site that is similar in most respects to the site being examined.

The use of regression techniques and linear programming is not recommended unless the local government is willing to allocate substantial personnel, funds, and time to collect, manipulate, and analyze the data.

An alternative, subjective, and less costly approach is to obtain the professional opinion of those whose income depends on estimating the intricacies of real estate markets. Although responses can be self-serving, the likely results of a more analytic approach may be ascertained by discussions with realtors. A time consuming analysis is unnecessary if there is general agreement that a particular project had no discernible impact on nearby property.

It should be again noted that even if a change in the selling price of land can be established, this provides no information on the aggregate, communitywide impact on property values. It may well be that a rise in value near the site is fully offset by a decline in those sites previously considered as potential locations for a project. For example, if a national corporation has decided to locate a large industrial facility at one of four intersections of an interstate highway in a county, the land value at all four intersections should increase about equally prior to the announced decision if all four sites are equal contenders. Once a decision has been made, land near the selected site should increase further in value, while the prices of land at the other three locations would presumably be reduced to their previous levels. This also suggests that persons most likely to gain from site-specific changes should undertake such analyses and not wait for the public sector to measure site-specific effects.

# IV. FINDINGS AND RECOMMENDATIONS

One tentative conclusion reached in this review is that the addition of low density, detached housing to a community increases the value of similar housing stock. Expansion of nonresidential development, particularly industrial facilities, can, but will not necessarily, have an adverse effect on the value of detached housing in communities where such housing is predominate. However, empirical evidence concerning the effects of new development on existing property values is limited. While the likely direction of effects is known, little is known about their magnitude.

Based on the literature review and the author's experience, local governments will find it difficult to assess the impact of specific new development on the values of both undeveloped land and existing structures at the community level. At best, a community can examine the effects on values of land in the immediate vicinity of large developments. From the jurisdiction's perspective, however, only communitywide effects, if any, are important. Given the limited nature of most methods for analyzing land value effects and of market property value data, communities should not invest substantial resources in this impact evaluation area. Any analysis undertaken should be a joint effort with assessment officials, since the results may be equally or more useful to these officials.

# GENERAL CONCLUSIONS

The major nonfiscal economic effects of development are changes in employment, income, housing, and property value, although each of the four areas also has a direct effect on the fiscal posture of a community. The quantity of information available at the local level to estimate these effects and the quality of analytic techniques differs in each of the areas.

Increasing employment opportunities for residents is a major and the frequently dominant factor community leaders cite in seeking to attract new development. Decisionmakers are often willing to endure adverse environmental or fiscal effects to increase employment levels. Despite the importance local officials attach to creating new jobs, the likely residence of those to be employed in a new facility, or the level of inmigration attributable to a new facility, is generally unknown. Similarly, limited hard data are available on the effects of new facilities on unemployed residents of the community. Thus, attempts by local government to improve job opportunities for its own residents may be only partially met through induced growth. It _is_ possible to estimate both the future level of direct employment and the payroll expansion that will result from _identified_ additional new commercial or industrial development. Some residents, particularly those providing goods and services, will benefit by increased economic activity, even if the share of jobs taken by local residents is small. Fiscal benefits may also accrue to the community, at least in the long run.

The demand for housing generated by additional employment depends primarily on the level of inmigration caused by the new facility. However, higher income, even in the absence of inmigration, can increase the demand for more expensive and/or more land-intensive housing. Inmigrants may select residences outside the boundaries of the community where they are employed. The choice of residence, in addition to employment accessibility (which benefits the community), depends on factors such as neighborhood amenities and local tax rates. Since a typical household takes seven to nine trips daily, most of which are not to or from the place of employment, accessibility of potential housing to shopping, schools, and recreation facilities is an important factor in the locational decision. Accessibility factors, however, can be dominated by different neighborhood amenities.

This report has focused on ways to determine if projected additional housing units will increase housing choices for local residents and satisfy unmet housing demand. Data on personal income, age distribution of households, and household size are necessary for estimating the type and price range of housing present residents are likely to seek. The application of methods to estimate these characteristics, and data on the relationship between housing and household characteristics discussed in this report, can provide at least rough estimates of the proportion of projected housing units within the financial resources of community residents. Since developers typically plan their houses for a regional rather than local market, new housing is frequently beyond the financial means of many local residents. As analytic models to predict household location are still in an early stage of development, and since their results are difficult to assess, local government should use less sophisticated techniques.

Higher real income for existing residents, the formation of new households, and net inmigration will increase the demand for housing and have a positive effect on the value of both undeveloped land and existing residential units. While little is known about how a specific development will affect the value of nearby property, low density, detached housing added to an area where such housing is already dominant tends to have a positive effect on existing housing values.

Four main conclusions have emerged from this examination. First, evaluations of employment and housing effects at the local level are useless without a concurrent analysis of employment and housing from the regional and metropolitan perspective. Property value changes must be considered at the neighborhood level as opposed to fiscal effects, which can be best evaluated within municipal boundaries.

Second, various land use, planning, and other models have had only limited success in assessing the impact of either individual or aggregate development. The use of these models is costly, and their verification usually requires surveys which can add substantially to this cost. The state of the art is not sufficiently advanced to justify the use of complex models by local personnel in any but the largest communities. The typical jurisdiction can apply its resources more efficiently by allocating funds to develop simple relationships and to conduct resident surveys.

Third, employment, income, and housing are very closely interrelated. Therefore, it is both efficient and prudent to examine these effects concurrently since a common data base was probably used. Given this, the examination of results will produce more usable information. While property values can be evaluated independently of employment, income, and housing, it is preferable to include such analyses as part of a broader economic impact study.

Finally, aggregate economic effects of individual developments at the local level are typically minor. Although some local residents benefit directly from almost any new development, the benefits do not necessarily accrue to the general population. Further, some residents, typically a minority, may be worse off. Therefore, it is useful for local governments to estimate, from the private and public sector perspective, not only the economic impact of individual and aggregate development but also the income distributive effects of growth on the local population.